CW01083502

MODELLING RAILWAY SCENERY

VOLUME 2

FIELDS, HEDGES AND TREES

RELATED TITLES FROM CROWOOD

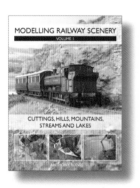

Modelling Railway Scenery Vol 1
Cuttings, Hills, Mountains, Streams and Lakes

ANTHONY REEVES

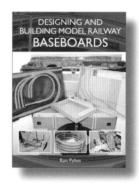

Designing and Building Model Railway Baseboards

RON PYBUS

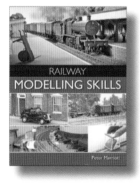

Railway Modelling Skills

PETER MARRIOTT

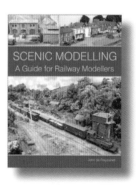

Scenic Modelling

JOHN DE FRAYSSINET

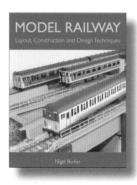

Model Railway Layout, Construction & Design Techniques

NIGEL BURKIN

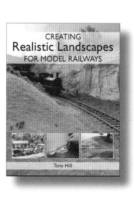

Creating Realistic Landscapes for Model Railways

TONY HILL

MODELLING RAILWAY SCENERY

VOLUME 2

FIELDS, HEDGES AND TREES

ANTHONY REEVES

THE CROWOOD PRESS

First published in 2015 by
The Crowood Press Ltd
Ramsbury, Marlborough
Wiltshire SN8 2HR

www.crowood.com

This impression 2018

© Anthony Reeves 2015

All rights reserved. No part of this publication may be reproduced or
transmitted in any form or by any means, electronic or mechanical,
including photocopy, recording, or any information storage and retrieval
system, without permission in writing from the publishers.

British Library Cataloguing-in-Publication Data
A catalogue record for this book is available from the British Library.

ISBN 978 1 84797 943 8

Dedication
For Nic, Luke, Libby and Benson and my family, past, present and future:
'Thank you for putting up with me and for your continued support, cheers!'

Acknowledgements
The author and publisher would like to thank the following companies for
their generous support in the making of this book: AK Interactive, Deluxe
Materials, Javis Manufacturing Ltd, Noch, TREEMENDUS. Special thanks to
Andy York and *BRM* magazine for the additional photography.

Disclaimer
The author and the publisher do not accept any responsibility in any
manner whatsoever for any error or omission, or any loss, damage, injury,
adverse outcome, or liability of any kind incurred as a result of the use
of any of the information contained in this book, or reliance upon it. If in
doubt about any aspect of scenic modelling, readers are advised to seek
professional advice.

Typeset in Gill Sans by Bookcraft Ltd, Stroud, Gloucestershire
Printed and bound in India by Replika Press Pvt. Ltd.

CONTENTS

LAND · SCAPE
/ˈlan(d) ˌskāp/

Noun: All the visible features of an area of countryside or land, often considered in terms of their aesthetic appeal.

Verb: Improve the aesthetic appearance of (a piece of land) by changing its contours, adding ornamental features and plantings.

INTRODUCTION – WHY LANDSCAPE?

Having been born in 1967, I missed out on the steam era of British railways. I grew up in a time of diesel and electric locomotives and have seen a number of the classes I grew up with disappear from service as they themselves are relegated to the history books.

One element of rail travel that does stay constant however, other than its seasonal change and the occasional intervention of man, is the countryside the trains pass through. I have always had a fascination with scenery and what it consists of both in the real world and in the scale model world. I have always studied the scenery and the structures railways run through and how the landscape, structures and railways have a profound effect on each other.

My passion for the scenic elements of railway modelling has encouraged me to develop the TREEMENDUS range of scenic modelling materials, which are used by modellers worldwide. This is my second book on the subject of how to accurately create convincing scale model scenery following *Modelling Railway Scenery Volume 1 – Cuttings, Hills, Mountains, Streams and Lakes* (Crowood, 2013). I hope this new publication brings you enjoyment and inspires you to improve your own scenic modelling skills.

For the many thousands of railway modellers in the UK, and indeed worldwide, it is the locomotives, rolling stock, permanent way and railway-related buildings that are the most important and interesting aspects of a model railway – and of course without these features there would be no railway at all.

'Playing with trains' has come a long way since the days of so-called 'carpet railways': these were essentially steam engines that ran directly on the floor without the use of a track. Table-top railways were later introduced, with clockwork and

Fig. 1: It's not difficult to see the attraction for railway modellers of recreating scenes like this in scale model form.

Fig. 2: By taking note of natural features in the real world our model railways can be made to look very lifelike.

then electric-powered locomotives running on primitive-looking, unrealistic track; the latter was an improvement on the previous clockwork engines, but the trains were still toy-like and used basic-looking accessories.

Today as advances are continually being made in the quality of almost all areas of railway modelling, with fantastically detailed stock and realistic digital sound commonplace in all the popular scales available, it is becoming more and more desirable to run railways through a landscape worthy of the trains themselves. As a wide choice of stock is readily available for almost every region and era of British railways, there are obvious reasons for wanting to

Fig. 3: Irwell Vale Halt, Irwell Vale, East Lancashire Railway, BL0 0QA (June 2013).

The East Lancashire Railway

The East Lancashire Railway is a heritage railway that spans two counties, Lancashire and Greater Manchester; it is situated in the northwest of England, and more commonly referred to as 'the East Lancs Railway'. The East Lancs Railway currently (May 2014) operates a 12-mile (19km) stretch of railway between Rawtenstall and Heywood, on which it runs a mixture of steam and diesel-hauled trains.

Fig. 4: Landscape features such as this small hawthorn are just waiting to be modelled.

faithfully re-create landscape which is recognizably typical of a particular region of the country, or even to copy the features of a chosen stretch of railway line as it appears in the real world.

In my first book *Modelling Railway Scenery Volume 1 – Cutting, Hills, Mountains, Streams and Lakes*, individual dioramas were made to show the various aspects of the landscape being modelled. *Modelling Railway Scenery Volume 2 – Fields, Hedges and Trees* is presented in a different way. In this book you are advised as to the best way to collect information from a particular location, which you can refer to at a later date; in this case I have studied a stretch of railway line running through Lancashire which is part of the East Lancashire Railway.

ABOUT THIS BOOK

The aim of this book is to guide the reader through the process of collecting photographic information and converting the information within the photographs, through the use of step-by-step demonstrations, into scale model scenic features for your own model railway layouts.

The book starts with a field trip on a sunny June day to the area surrounding Irwell Vale Halt, a small station on the East Lancs Railway. Whilst on the field trip a huge amount of colour reference photographs were taken, and these photographs served as reference to the colour, shape and size of the scenic features in the area, as well as the important smaller details that make up the scenes in the photographs; many of the photographs can be seen in the following chapters.

The important features of the landscape are recreated in step-by-step format using readily available scenic modelling materials with accompanying full colour photographs of both the prototype and the various stages of creating a scale model version. Although *Modelling Railway Scenery Volume 2* is aimed at 1:76 scale, or 'OO' modellers, the various techniques and materials can be used for most of the commonly modelled scales – the principles of creating the scenic features are the same, it is a simple matter of scaling the size of the hedges, trees and so on up or down to complement the scale of the rolling stock and buildings that appear on the layout.

Using the scenic features created throughout the book a scale model representation of the field trip photographs is created in the form of a 3 by 2ft (90 by 60cm) diorama. The diorama is not intended to be an exact copy of one particular photograph from the field trip: it simply includes many of the landscape features found around this particular stretch of East Lancs Railway, and it is these features that will give the model all the charm and character of that particular area.

THE FIELD TRIP

Taking a field trip to the area you have chosen to model is a perfect way to become familiar with the characteristic features of the surrounding landscape and how the railway interacts with them. If at all possible it is highly advisable to take a train journey through the area during the time of year on which your layout will be based, as this will enable you to get a close-up view of the track-side features and beyond into the neighbouring scenery.

Whilst on your field trip take as many colour photographs as possible, and make notes on the scenic features of the landscape – for instance, the approximate length of the grass in the fields, the size of the hedgerows, and what kind of plant life they are made up of. It may also be advantageous to record the approximate height, and if possible the species, of the trees that are growing in and around the area, as it is these trees, along with the buildings, that will add the all-important height to your model railway scenery.

It is true that some of the information you record may serve no real purpose to you at all once you return home, but there are bound to be some images that illustrate what you are looking for perfectly, and it is these photographs that will be the reference from which you work for a long time to come.

It is also useful to take some photographs of the area from a distance if possible, as these photographs will give you a good indication of what the surrounding area should look like when scaled down in model form.

This book sets out to recreate a beautiful rural landscape, and as such contains mostly photographs that feature natural scenic features; but even if you are planning a layout based in an urban or industrial setting, a field trip is still a worthwhile and often enjoyable part of the research process.

MATERIALS

The majority of the construction and groundwork materials that are used during the course of this book are readily available, lightweight and fairly inex-

pensive. Each of the individual scenic features has an accompanying materials list that will help you to have all the relevant materials and tools to hand before you start a particular project.

CONSTRUCTION MATERIALS

The term 'construction materials' refers to all the materials used to create the actual rises and falls that may be present in the landscape. These might include railway cuttings, embankments, hillsides, cliffs and other small landscape features. Construction materials are usually eventually hidden from view as they are generally covered with groundwork materials. The construction materials used to create the 3 by 2ft (90 by 60cm) diorama built at the end of the book include chipboard, timber, screws, PVA glue, polystyrene/kingspan, cocktail sticks and cork sheet. Some of these construction materials can be substituted with other materials, and where possible alternative suggestions are given.

GROUNDWORK MATERIALS

The term 'groundwork materials' refers to the scenic modelling materials used to create the realistic and visually impressive landscape our trains run through – grass, hedges, trees, vegetation, weeds, paths and all the other features that are added to the visible landscape. Groundwork materials include ballast, fur fabric, static grass fibres, rubberized horsehair, tree-making materials, scatters and earth powders.

The groundwork materials used in the making of the diorama come from the TREEMENDUS scenic modelling materials range. There is a huge range of scenic modelling materials on the market, and I will also be incorporating some of these materials into the groundwork as its construction commences.

TOOLS

A basic toolkit is required – an electric drill and a jigsaw are an invaluable addition to the railway room, as are sharp scissors, a sharp scalpel or craft knife, a steel rule, wire cutters, assorted paintbrushes and paints. A plastic bottle with a nozzle and an atomizer attachment is useful for ballasting and groundwork in

Fig. 5: A view of Ramsbottom station, East Lancs Railway.

general. Hairspray is also a very useful 'tool', and is used in abundance in association with groundwork materials and scenic glue, although it is advisable to keep it away from your metal rails.

Reference is given in the text of each chapter to the specific tools required to complete the landscape feature being created. The modelling techniques involved vary according to whether fields, hedges or trees are being created, but there is also some repetition throughout the chapters. Readers are alerted to the fact that the same techniques have been used elsewhere in the book: this is done with the aim of inspiring consistency in an individual's scenic modelling.

HISTORICAL BACKGROUND

We know that the railways were built through the existing landscape. Sometimes the landscape could be used to advantage, while at others it caused great problems, necessitating the construction of huge viaducts and tunnels, for example. There was a time when the railways transported produce and people to many rural towns in the UK, areas much like the one being modelled in this book. Many small, unprofitable lines were unceremoniously closed after the 1963

and 1965 reports by Dr Richard Beeching, known as the Beeching cuts or Beeching axe. The first report referred to the 'reduction of route network and restructuring of the railways in Great Britain', which resulted in 55 per cent of stations and 30 per cent of route miles in the UK being lost for ever. Heritage railways such as the East Lancs Railway keep some of these otherwise long-forgotten lines open today, and far from completely vanishing, some of them are once again carrying passengers and making a profit.

With a little careful planning our model railways can be built to look as if they, too, have been incorporated into the existing landscape. We can use some of the features of the landscape to our advantage, especially when we include tall, dense trees to help disguise exit points into fiddle yards 'off stage' for example.

Of course field trips are less necessary if you are intending to build a model railway that runs through a generic landscape, but nonetheless it is still well worth taking the time to pay a visit to some actual railway lines, and photographing them if possible to get a feel for the colours nature has to offer, and the way the railway, hedges, fences, trees, fields and other scenic features interact with each other and the surrounding landscape in general.

Fig. 6: Light can have a huge effect on the way we see colour, both in nature and on our models.

COLOUR VALUES

We know that the fields, hedges and trees in any landscape change with the coming and going of the seasons, and the weather on any given day can have a massive effect on how everything in the landscape appears. The choice of season being modelled will have a great influence on the colour values used in the scenery on the layout; these colour values tell the story and give the viewer an indication of the time of year being presented in the scene before them. The amount of colour you include in your scenic modelling is a personal choice, as we all perceive colour differently. This is what thankfully makes our layouts original and unique. Don't attempt to copy other people's model railways, but try to emulate what you see in real life.

If you can't get to the location you are planning to base your own scenery on, then this shouldn't present too much of a problem. We are fortunate that nowadays we have at our fingertips a huge amount of information on almost any subject. The age of the computer has really transformed everything we do and the speed at which we do it. During the course of building your model railway, even armed with a multitude of field-trip photographs and notes, there may be times when you need to refer to the internet for information, whether written or visual – and be sure to make the most of this valuable asset. In some cases all that remains of certain places are historical photographs, and these can be a very welcome resource indeed, especially if they are all that remains of a particular station, for example.

SUMMARY

To summarize, the first chapter of this book describes a field trip to Irwell Vale Halt on the East Lancs Railway, a photographic bonanza whilst on location. The chapters that follow are a series of step-by-step demonstrations showing how to create the various scenic elements that can be seen in the photographs. Finally, all the elements of the landscape are brought together in the creation of a complete model of the railway running through natural-looking scenery based on the landscape captured in the field-trip photograph.

Fig. 7: All aboard?

CHAPTER ONE

FIELD TRIP TO IRWELL VALE HALT

Fig. 8: Beware of trains.

> ## Warning!
>
> It is vitally important to remember that railways can be very dangerous places: they always have been and always will be, so take care when on location doing your field trip research. Always ask permission if possible from the respective landowner where necessary, and be sure to bin your rubbish and leave the location how you found it.

Photographs and written notes are probably the best way of recording the major scenic features of the landscape, as well as all the smaller yet equally important details you see on your field trip. Digital cameras have made recording field trips so easy, as they enable us to take literally hundreds of images in a single day. On arriving home we can upload the images to a computer, sort them into a suitable filing system for easy retrieval in the future – in this case 'Fields', 'Hedges' and 'Trees' – and can zoom in and out to look more closely at the individual features in a frame. It is also quick and easy to send them to other people via email should you need a second opinion on something, or wish to show them something you saw on your travels.

Note that the amount of natural light available on the day of your field trip plays an important part in, and has an enormous effect on, the quality and colour values of your photographs. For obvious reasons, it is probably more desirable to choose a bright and sunny day for your field trip – though as we all know, it is almost impossible to second guess the British weather!

EAST LANCS RAILWAY PHOTOGRAPHS

As discussed, the following photographs and accompanying notes were all taken on a field trip to the East Lancs Railway. Although the photographs are used for reference in the step-by-step projects, I was not intending to use any one particular photograph on which to base my landscape, but merely to take inspiration from the colours and textures in the photographs to create a scene with all the flavour of the Irwell Vale.

Fig. 9 shows an Irwell Vale station sign fixed to a short length of unpainted wooden fencing. The sign is actually made up from two halves joined vertically down the centre of the sign. The sign is surrounded by honeysuckle and *Euonymus* (spindle trees). For the diorama I have in mind for this book there will in fact be no station, but this photograph shows the huge variety of plants growing to the rear of station platforms.

Fig. 10 shows the type of scenery that looks great in scale model form. To the rear of the station platform and running all the way down the track there is a dense row of tall trees, including silver birch, sycamore and beech. A row of trees like this will

Fig. 9: Irwell Vale station sign.

give a dramatic look to the rear of a diorama or layout. To the front of the track on a low embankment grow tall grass and weeds, including rosebay willowherb – though this is not yet in flower in the photograph. Note how the fence separating the field in the foreground from the small embankment is almost invisible, as it is engulfed by the tall plants on the embankment and the weeds and tall grasses in the field.

Fig. 10: Irwell Vale sits in beautiful countryside, and this type of scenery looks great in scale model form.

Fig. 11: 80080 arrives at Irwell Vale.

Before leaving the station to gather more reference photographs, BR Standard Class 4 2–6–4MT No. 80080 arrived, hauling a short train consisting of three carriages. Fig. 11 lends some reference to the scale of the trees behind the platform. It also shows well how the grass growing along the fence has been allowed to grow untrimmed.

In Fig. 12 an earth path runs along a river down to the underpass that takes pedestrians beneath the track. The grass in the fields along the track is kept fairly short by the constant grazing of sheep. The hawthorn to the right of the track makes a good feature; it is just on the bottom of the embankment and not in the field. Note, too, how the grass along

Fig. 12: A path leads down to the small underpass.

Fig. 13: A huge range of tones and textures can be seen here.

the track grows into the ballast. The trees to the left of the photograph are a continuation of the row of trees behind the platform, although here they tend to thin out a little.

Fig. 13 shows just how different colours and textures can appear even in the same field. The tufts are prominent, growing from the very short grass that typifies the majority of the field. The grass around the edge of the field is longer and contains a fair mixture of weeds and other plants. The tufts are as tall as the sheep.

Bordering this part of the field there are drystone walls and fences running adjacent to each other. Note the stile in the corner of the field, a nice detail to add to any countryside fence or wall. The old oak tree stands all alone (Fig. 14) and is therefore

Fig. 14: A stunning old oak tree stands alone.

Fig. 15: A variety of trees stand towards the rear of this scene.

very rounded in shape due to the abundance of light it receives from all directions. It is fairly open in texture, too.

A row of assorted trees showing a huge variety in both colour and texture runs along the far side of the tracks (Fig. 15). Thick ground-cover vegetation grows even underneath the trees along this stretch of railway. Note the almost dead tree to the left-hand side of the photo. Two light green saplings now grow in what would once have been its shade.

Small trees grow on the near side of the track (Fig. 16). A high visibility overall adds colour to the greenery of the trees. Note the difference in both colour and texture between the two types of grasses growing on either side of the drystone walls.

Fig. 16: Two small, very different trees stand in front of the railway line. Note the track being checked.

Fig. 17: This photograph shows the several shades of green and the textural difference between the trees and grasses in the area.

In Fig. 17 a Deltic is dwarfed by the trees to the rear of the track and hidden from view by the trees on the near side of the track. The lushest, greenest grass tends to grow on each side of the path that runs along the wall bordering the railway line. The grass in the rest of the field in front of the wall tends to be long and full of tufts, with obvious colour variation.

In Fig. 18 the train disappears behind trees on the near side of the track as it runs out of view; this may be useful for disguising traffic entering a fiddle yard. This photograph has a great deal of valuable information in it – and note how much the background hills and sky resemble readily available pre-printed back scenes.

Fig. 18: This is exactly the type of scene that offers plenty of scenic possibilities to modellers.

In Fig. 19, note how the sides of the rails are actually almost the same colour as the sleepers, as opposed to being a bright rust colour. Of course this does vary and is a noteworthy detail. The ballast directly beneath the rails is also slightly discoloured, and the individual sleepers vary somewhat in colour. The sleeper to the left has a layer of ballast covering it.

Fig. 20 shows a beautiful silver birch tree that grows next to the path on the side away from the wall. Note its open structure and how its branches grow in relation to the hillside to the right of it, mirroring the angle of the slope.

In Fig. 21 a row of trees stands behind a simple fence. The fence here consists of wooden posts and just two thin wires running horizontally along the posts, the wires held in place with simple 'U'-shaped nails. The scene is characterized by many different tones of green, and a fair number of dead branches, too. In the field there are long tufts, docks, thistles and other weeds growing.

Fig. 19: A close-up study of the track and ballast colours.

Fig. 20: Silver birch with a very open foliage structure.

Fig. 21: Some trees naturally show a large proportion of their trunk, whilst some show none at all.

Fig. 22 shows a mature sycamore tree in full leaf standing just behind the new fence. The fence is constructed using rounded, pole-like wooden posts and wire; some of the fence posts are far from vertical. In the foreground can be seen the remains of an old, weathered fence that once enclosed the field. It was built using square-edged wooden posts.

The very mature sycamore tree, depicted in Fig. 23, growing next to the river is a little way from the railway, but is a typical example of the size and style of the trees to be seen in the area. Note how low down its branches start obscuring its entire trunk. Around its base grow a variety of grasses, weeds and wild flowers.

Fig. 22: Note the tiny remains of the original fence in the foreground.

Fig. 23: A well-proportioned, mature sycamore.

Another old sycamore tree grows alongside the river, as depicted in Fig. 24. This time some of its lower trunk can be seen, as it has no low-growing branches. Some of the branches growing further up the trunk can be seen through the open canopy of leaves. Note, too, the size and colour of the stones at the edge of the river: this stone colour is typical of the area and will be used wherever rocks are visible on the layout. The river itself at this point is fairly shallow and there are signs of rippling as the water runs over the rocks on the river bed.

Fig. 25 shows a general view of the type of landscape around Irwell Vale. Note the various tufts and weeds growing in the field and the variety in the colour of the grasses. In front of the row of trees stands a simple fence made with rounded wooden

Fig. 24: Solitary trees often develop an even, rounded growth formation.

Fig. 25: This photograph shows many of the details worth including in any model landscape.

posts. The dense foliage and assorted colours of the trees serve as a useful backdrop to the scene, and there are also a few dead or dying trees among the living ones.

The track runs over an underpass. To the left-hand side of the underpass long grass borders the track, while to the right can be seen the start of a stone wall (Fig. 26). Note how the ballast spreads from the sleepers to the wall, and how short grass grows through it.

In Fig. 27 small weeds can be seen growing along the base of the wall. The pillars of the underpass wall are capped with heavy coping stones. Note how well grazed the field in the background is: the grass appears to be very short.

Fig. 28 depicts a few hawthorns and small shrubs that run along the embankment on the opposite side to the row of trees. Note the trunk of the hawthorn is completely obscured by foliage.

Fig. 29 shows a close-up of the railway line with its well weathered wooden sleepers. Note the weathering of the ballast, too, and the variety of colour present in the ballast. This photograph gives a good visual example of the shoulder of ballast as it falls away to the wall of the underpass.

Fig. 30 shows the type of landscape surrounding Irwell Vale. The long grass in the corner of the field makes way for the much shorter grass and tufts in the main field. A mix of drystone walling and fence separates one field from another. Telegraph poles are evident carrying cables over the fields.

Fig. 26: Longer grass skirts the track side.

Fig. 27: Thick slabs of stone cap the pillars on the underpass. Note how short the well-grazed grass in the distant field appears.

Fig. 28: A fantastic-looking line-side hawthorn and other small trees grow along the track.

Fig. 29: A good reference to the colour of the rails, sleepers and ballast.

Fig. 30: A great overall photograph of the type of landscape surrounding Irwell Vale.

Fig. 31: There are plenty of details on this overgrown embankment worthy of modelling.

Fig. 32: This photograph shows how the ballast and the short and long grasses blend together.

The image in Fig. 31 really captures all the elements I want to include in the layout, both in colour and texture. The fence running along the embankment is almost totally obscured by vegetation. One of the trees has its lower trunk visible whilst others have their trunks obscured. Long and short grasses run along the embankment and are peppered with colourful wild flowers, and an immense range of foliage colours and textures blend together to give fluidity to the landscape.

In this photograph (Fig. 32) note how the ballast in front of the platform is much more weathered than the ballast shown in Fig. 29 (which is on the approach to the station), and also how the sleepers have changed from weathered wooden sleepers to more modern concrete ones. The grass growing at the side of the track yellows where it meets the ballast. Note also the dark oily line running parallel with the right-hand rail. Details like this don't have to be added, but can bring extra realism to your layout.

Note that in this general view (Fig. 33), some of the grasses growing on the right-hand side of the tracks are growing almost up to the rails. This is another image that captures many of the elements that give this stretch of line its character.

Fig. 33: It's said a picture is worth a thousand words.

Fig. 34: A great case of perspective in action, both of the carriages and the trees on the hillside.

Fig. 35: Sheep are an important feature of the landscape, and also give an indication of the scale of the natural features.

Creating perspective in our models is a useful way of tricking the eye. In Fig. 34, note that as the carriages get smaller, so do the trees in the background.

Another good example of perspective is shown in Fig. 35, in the difference in size of the sheep between those in the foreground and those in the distance. The grass is very short in the field, and although not visible in the photograph the surface of the field is peppered with small stones which are the same in appearance as those found in and around the river.

In Fig. 36 a solitary tree casts an almost circular shadow on the grass beneath it; sheep gather in the shade to avoid the midday sun. The tufts in the field are approximately two to three feet (about 70cm) tall; in particular note the variety of colours even in the same groups of tufts. The grey slate rooftops just visible over the edge of the hillside make an interesting feature amongst the green of the fields.

The image in Fig. 37 depicts the fence behind the station which has been stained brown as opposed to painted white; it shows different tones and is not a uniform colour. Vegetation grows along some of its length.

Fig. 36: Note the colour variation in the tufts.

Fig. 37: Take photographs of everything: you may need them one day.

Fig. 38: Simple creosote-stained fencing. Note how the plants grow along the bottom of the fence over the edge of the platform.

In Fig. 38 the plants growing at the rear of the station have naturally spread to the platform and taken root along the fence.

Fig. 39 shows that the grass growing along the track side is fairly high; a couple of conifers are growing just behind the fence on the embankment. This short length of fence consists of vertical concrete posts with four metal poles running horizontally through them. A small line-side sign stands in the distance.

In Fig. 40, note the colour variation on the hollow trunk of the old oak tree. The tree itself is still growing healthily, although characteristically a few old boughs and branches that have long fallen from it lie on the floor around it. Grass grows around

Fig. 39: A couple of conifers have established themselves just beyond the boundary fence.

Fig. 40: The hollow trunk of an oak just up the hill opposite the station.

Fig. 41: Just the subtlest splash of colour will add interest to our scenic modelling.

these so that only the branches that are above it are visible.

In Fig. 41, small splashes of colour from flowering weeds and wild flowers growing among the general greens of the embankment add interest to the overall appearance of the landscape.

In Fig. 42, tall grasses can be seen growing alongside the track; note the colour difference in the rails in the background.

As in nature, not everything man-made is perfectly straight and square. In Fig. 43, note the angle of the telegraph pole in relation to the fence posts behind.

Fig. 42: A bit of yellow adds the colour here.

Fig. 43: Note that not all telegraph poles, even in the real world, are perfectly upright.

Fig. 44: Line-side features can also add a splash of colour amongst all the greenery.

The image in Fig. 44 depicts the huge variety of textures and colours that border the railway here. The post of the signal is particularly rusty.

WRITTEN NOTES

As well as taking photographic references it is also prudent to make written notes about certain features around the railway line, especially if you intend to recreate a faithful study of the area. Usually simple notes, just like the notes accompanying the photographs on the previous pages, are enough to remind you how things actually were on the day. For instance, how tall are the hedgerows and trees? What colour is the ballast? How tall and what colour are the grass and weeds running along the track? Where did the crop finish in relation to the hedges surrounding the field, and what was the visual difference between the two? Was there a path across a certain field, and if so, where did it go – did it cross a stile?

NOTES – Trackside

The grass along the track grows right into the ballast, even up to the sleepers in some places, it tends to yellow where it borders the ballast. Along the boundary fence tall grasses and weeds grow, almost totally obscuring the fence from view.

Fig. 45: Written notes can be just as important as photographs.

Of course, all the above questions will probably be answered in the photographs you take, but the notes will serve as a reminder of the things you actually went on the field trip to search for in the first place.

CHAPTER TWO

SHORT GRASS EFFECTS

Fig. 46: A wonderful image showing the very short grass in front of Irwell Vale Halt.

In rural areas of the country fields make up a huge percentage of the landscape, and they can vary enormously in appearance. Some of them contain livestock and are well grazed, or they are situated in an environment where the weather or surroundings naturally stop the grass from growing and it appears very short, as in some of the fields in the reference photographs. Others are left to grow wild and can be full of weeds, grasses, brambles and so forth. Many of the fields we see are used for crops of one kind or another, and their appearance can change drastically over the course of a year.

There are various methods of effectively modelling short grass, from a simple covering of fine scatters to the use of static grass fibres and fur fabrics. The following demonstrations, using the various materials, will guide you through the steps required to achieve the best results from each material.

SCATTERS

Materials

- Aerosol or emulsion paint
- Diluted PVA glue
- Assorted scatters
- Earth Powder
- Small stones

Tools

- Paintbrush
- Sieve (optional)

One of the simplest ways of creating short grass for model railway layouts and dioramas is to use very fine groundwork scatters. The scatters used here are very fine and therefore perfect for the creation of very short, well grazed grass, or areas of grass where the local conditions will not allow it to grow well. It is advisable to use more than one colour scatter otherwise the covering will end up being an unrealistic monotone.

Whether scatters are used on a flat surface or a pre-shaped hillside, it is always advisable to give the surface of the terrain a coat of paint: this ensures that any small areas that may show through the scatter will appear as realistic earth colour showing through the grass. Match pots of matt emulsion are one of the best options as they are good value for money, are readily available from local DIY stores, have good coverage, and are available in a huge range of tones. Paint sprayed directly from a tin is also a quick and easy method of covering the baseboard. Mid to dark brown paints are recommended for general earth, but subtle green tones can also be used, as can more reddish clay colours, and even chalky white if the local conditions call for it.

In Fig. 47, the paint used to cover this small piece of board was applied directly from an aerosol tin. Be sure to mask the area around where you are painting with sheets of newspaper to prevent the paint getting on other parts of the scene or track. The coat of paint needn't be thick, just enough to cover the surface. One coat is usually enough, and it should be allowed to dry.

Before adding the scatter and in order to hold it in place, paint a layer of glue over the painted surface of the landscape. Mix your own glue, in order to achieve the correct consistency and fixing abilities: to this end use PVA. Dilute the PVA in a ratio of approximately three parts water to one part glue: the best way to do this is to put the water and PVA into a plastic bottle with a lid and shake the two together, mixing them thoroughly; then pour the glue into a container wide enough to allow you to dip a paintbrush into it. Use a wide paintbrush (see Fig. 48) to paint the glue over the pre-painted surface, and be sure to apply it in a thick layer as this will help the various applications of scatter to adhere to the surface.

The first layer of scatter to be used in this example is Spring Green, and it must be applied to the landscape whilst the glue is still wet. For small areas it can be applied by hand using small pinches carefully sprinkled over the glue; for areas that require larger quantities it is advisable to apply it through a sieve (see Fig. 49). Using a sieve allows more control, thus

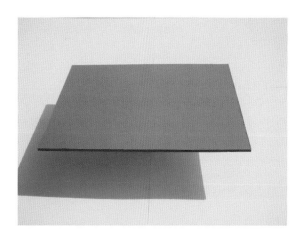

Fig. 47: Matt emulsion paint gives a simple base on which to add scatter.

Fig. 48: Diluted PVA glue, applied with a paintbrush, will hold the scatter firmly in place.

ensuring a fairly even coverage of scatter over the field so that a maximum number of granules will come into contact with the glue, helping them to stick.

To achieve subtle colour variations to the surface of the field it is advisable to add further tones of fine scatter; this can also be applied all over the field using the sieve method. However, if your secondary colour, in this example Midsummer Green, is to be used in only specific areas of the field – for instance only around the central part, or around the edges or in random small patches – it is best applied by hand in small pinches, adding a bit at a time. Small areas of diluted PVA glue are allowed to drip from a paintbrush in the spots where you want the darker patches to be (see Fig. 50).

Finally, whilst the glue is still wet, a third tone of scatter is introduced to the surface of the field; this will add to the realistic appearance. Here I am using Late Summer fine scatter, applying it by hand in little pinches (see Fig. 51). This scatter gives the impression of dry or dead grass and can be applied in small, randomly shaped patches. It is also effective when added along well trodden paths and underneath hedges and bushes, as it gives the impression of the kind of dry grass sometimes found in these places.

Some of the fields around Irwell Vale have tiny pale grey stones and small rocks showing through the surface, especially where the grass is well grazed and very thin, allowing the earth below to show through. To replicate this, add small patches of TREEMENDUS Earth Powder to the surface of the field. The Earth Powder will fall in between the granules of scatter and will soak up the glue used to hold the scatter in place. If it doesn't, then add a few drops of the diluted PVA glue using a paintbrush, and carefully apply the earth.

Fig. 49: Larger quantities of scatter may be applied with the aid of a sieve.

Fig. 50: Highlights of scatter are best applied in small quantities by hand.

Fig. 51: The application of varied tones of scatter will improve the look of the field.

Fig. 52: Small rocks of a suitable colour add to the natural appearance of the field's surface.

Fig. 53: Close-up image of a grazed field of short grass created using fine scatters.

On top of the earth apply tiny 'stones': I am using TREEMENDUS Limestone Scree to capture the look of the prototype photo; pale grey ballast would work well, too. Slightly larger rocks can be positioned individually by hand to give an aesthetically pleasing arrangement (see Fig. 52). A very light sprinkling of one of the green scatters may be necessary to help blend the various materials together.

Summary

Scatters provide a very simple and effective way of modelling fields with very short grass. A paintbrush for applying the glue and a sieve for applying the scatter are the only tools that are required. Three or more different-coloured scatters will add realism and variety to the grass in the field, and an optional application of earth and small stones will complete the scene. Choose a colour of stone to reflect the area you are modelling.

Fig. 54: Prototype image of a field containing patches of different-coloured grass. Static grass can be used to replicate grass such as this.

STATIC GRASS

Materials

- Cement
- Emulsion paint
- Earth Powder
- Scatter
- Static grass fibres
- Glue

Tools

- Paintbrush
- Static grass applicator

Static grass fibres are useful where an impression of slightly longer grasses is required. The fibres are applied to a layer of glue painted directly on to the surface of the baseboard, much like the scatters above, but this time the fibres are statically charged in an applicator as they are applied to the glue. The charge causes the fibres to leave the applicator in an upright position, and to 'stand' vertically in the glue.

As with scatter, for the most realistic results it is best to blend static grass fibres.

Rather than simply painting the baseboard using matt emulsion paint, as with the scatters, here the baseboard is given a coat of texture first (see Fig. 55). This textured coat is optional and simply removes the absolute flatness of a bare baseboard. Of course this texturing layer can also be used in conjunction with scatters.

The textured layer is a blend of cement, Earth Powder, medium scatter and PVA glue diluted three to one with water; 25 per cent of each material will give you a good texture to work with. Apply the mixture using a paintbrush, and stipple the surface as it dries to create even more texture. Be sure to wash out the brush with water after applying the textured layer, as you should each time you use a material containing PVA.

The surface of the textured layer can be further enhanced by painting it with various tones of earth-coloured paint (see Fig. 56); this is especially important if white plaster is used to add the texture, as the groundwork below the fibres is sometimes visible through them. Using two or more tones of emulsion paint gives some variety to the colour of the groundwork on which the fibres stand. Allow the paint to dry.

Fig. 55: Adding a texture to the baseboard can help improve the overall effect of the grass.

Fig. 56: Painting the texture with emulsion paints can add variation to the baseboard beneath the grass.

Fig. 57: Glue is applied to the baseboard texture. The glue holds the fibres in place.

Fig. 58: The shortest, brighter green fibres are put in place first.

Add the glue to the textured coating using a wide brush. Static grass manufacturers and suppliers recommend special static grass glue, as this causes the fibres to stand more vertically as they fall into the glue (see Fig. 57). Whilst static grass glue is obviously excellent at holding the fibres in place, a thick layer of ordinary PVA glue can be used as an alternative. A metal hook or nail is screwed or hammered into the surface, directly through the glue, and the crocodile clip attached to the applicator is clipped to the hook.

Begin by turning on the applicator. The first fibres to be put in place are the short, bright green ones (see Fig. 58). They are applied with the aid of a Noch Gras-master applicator, which gives the fibres their static charge. I generally apply an overall light base coverage using these short, bright green fibres; then fibres of differing tones and lengths can be applied in between whilst the glue is still wet.

The next step is to apply more fibres to the glue. Here (Fig. 59), fibres with a darker tone are

Fig. 59: Secondly, darker and slightly longer fibres are added.

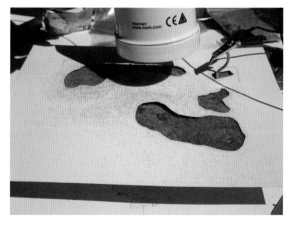

Fig. 60: Thirdly, the longest and palest fibres are added in small patches.

Fig. 61: Earth Powder sprinkled among the fibres will hide any shine from the glue.

Fig. 62: This close-up image shows the static grass field and the fibres standing upright.

being added, which are slightly longer than the ones applied previously. For the best results place these fibres more randomly, with small or large patches of darker green grasses growing through the shorter, brighter ones. To create small patches of grass, use the correct nozzle as supplied with your applicator.

Another way of creating small patches is to cut a sheet of paper or card so that it covers the area of your field, then cut or rip small apertures in it in the places where you want the patches to appear. The paper can then be placed back in position over the field allowing the static grass fibres to be added to the field in these positions. Lush grass may grow in dips in the terrain where there is a build-up of water, these puddles promoting a very healthy growth rate.

The third and final application of fibres comes next, again using the Gras-master applicator. These fibres are slightly longer still, and you should refer to the manufacturer's instructions as to which fittings to use in order to get the best result. Like the fibres applied in the last step, these paler fibres work well placed in small clumps (see Fig. 60), but they also work well when used as a general covering among the shorter brighter fibres, as they tone the overall look of the field. To 'plant' them in the field as small patches use the 'paper mask' method described above (see Fig. 60).

Sometimes the glue that holds the fibres in place reflects the light from beneath the fibres, especially if they have been applied only fairly thinly on the ground, causing an unwanted shine. A light sprinkling of Earth Powder will stick to the glue and resolve the problem (see Fig. 61). If possible tap the board around the field to ensure the Earth Powder falls down amongst the fibres and into the glue. Fine scatter can also be used to add further colour variation and texture to the field. Once the glue has dried completely, remove any loose fibres using a vacuum cleaner.

Summary

Static grass fibres provide another fairly simple way of modelling short grass. Applying a layer of terrain texture is optional, but does add to the effect. A paintbrush is used to add the glue to the landscape, but this time rather than applying the fibres with an ordinary sieve, a static grass applicator is used – basically a sieve that is being electrically charged as the fibres fall from it.

Fig. 63: An incredible variation of colour and texture are evident in this field. Note the piles of dried cut grass.

RAW GRASS

Raw Grass is teddy-bear fur fabric.

Materials

- Raw Grass (fur fabric)
- Green acrylic paints
- PVA

Tools

- Scissors
- Comb/hairbrush

A very versatile method of creating short grass for the fields on our model railway layouts is to use teddy-bear fur fabric. Fur fabric can be trimmed to length and coloured to match a particular season or style of grass. Once the fabric has been trimmed to fit its place on the layout, the fibres and fabric can be trimmed and coloured away from the layout. Neat PVA glue can be used to hold it in place on the baseboard when it is ready to 'plant'.

Refinements and detail can be made to the grass once it is in position on the layout: for instance, trimming pathways into it can add an extra feature to the field.

Whereas the two previous demonstrations concentrate on adding materials to the layout, building up the layers of colour and texture, this method initially requires removing fibres from the fabric sheet in order to form the various lengths of grass that will appear in the field.

First, the fibres on the sheet must be combed or brushed so they are standing upright. Then take a sharp pair of scissors and carefully trim the fibres to a length that suits the scheme and scale of grass you have in mind (see Fig. 64). It is best to trim the fibres working from different directions to avoid making 'tram lines' in the field. Keep all the trimmings for use elsewhere on the layout – they are particularly useful for hiding the edges of the Raw Grass sheet after it is glued to the baseboard.

Once the fibres on the sheet have been trimmed to length the grass is coloured to make it more realistic. Sap Green acrylic paint is used to colour this sheet. The paint is diluted with water, in this instance six parts water to one part paint: this results in a realistic-looking, mid-toned green grass which can be highlighted as work progresses. The diluted

Fig. 64: The fibres on the sheet can be trimmed with scissors to a length that simulates the type of grass being modelled.

Fig. 65: The fibres are easily coloured to suit the type of grass being modelled. Here, Sap Green acrylic paint is used.

paint is applied to the sheet in small drops from a bottle with a nozzle attached (see Fig. 65). The spots of paint are then rubbed into the fibres by hand to disperse them, and then the fibres are combed to disperse the paint even more. The sheet can be put to one side and allowed to dry. The paint should be applied only very lightly, and the sheet will then dry within thirty minutes.

Naturally during the process of trimming, the grass in certain areas of the sheet will have slightly longer or shorter fibres than the remainder of the sheet. To add highlights of colour to the field, some of these longer tufts can be picked out with green paint. Hooker's Green acrylic paint is used to high-light the longer tufts in this field, although any green paint will work. Dry-brushing the undiluted paint on to the fibres is a good way of building up the colour (see Fig. 66).

To do this, squeeze out a small amount of Hooker's Green paint on to a sheet of paper. Dip the tips of the bristles of a stiff brush into the paint, but then remove most of the paint from the brush by wiping it on a piece of tissue, leaving only a little paint on the bristle tips. Work the brush over the tufts of longer fibres on the sheet: this will add just a small amount of paint to the fibres, which is just enough to highlight them, therefore adding some variation to

the grasses of the field. By dry-brushing a variety of green and yellow paints over the field a very realistic and varied surface can be created.

Once the sheet has dried it can be glued to the baseboard using PVA glue. The glue is applied to the baseboard using a brush and *can* be diluted one part glue to one part water. Use your fingers to push the field down into the glue, making sure the backing

Fig. 66: Dry-brushing assorted tones of paint on to the sheet will add to the impression of the variety of grasses in the field.

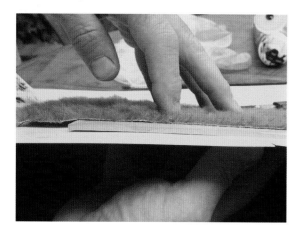

Fig. 67: Press the sheet into the glue to ensure it sticks to the baseboard.

Fig. 68: It is easy to add a path to the field even when the sheet is glued to the baseboard.

sheet is pressed firmly into it; this will help the grass adhere to the glue (see Fig. 67).

Often the perimeter of fields both in the real world and in model form are surrounded by some kind of physical barrier such as a fence, wall or hedge. These barriers will help hide the edge of the fabric sheet fairly easily. However, where the edges of the sheet may remain visible, across a gateway for instance, it is necessary to disguise the edge of the sheet where it joins the baseboard.

One way of doing this is to use the fibres that were collected by the brush (or comb) earlier. Trim the fibres into tiny short lengths to create the texture of a very fine fluff. This fluff is excellent at hiding the edge of the sheet after it has been glued down. Paint a little diluted PVA glue along the edge of the sheet, and carefully work the chopped fibres into the glue. Once the glue dries, the transition from the fibres on the sheet to the surrounding landscape will be seamless.

Trimming a path in the field is another way of further enhancing it, and can be done either before or after the grass has been glued in place. To make a path, take a sharp pair of scissors and trim away a narrow groove out of the fabric (see Fig. 68). The surface of the path can be covered with a material that reflects the conditions and geology of the land-scape being modelled. Note here how virtually all

the fibres have been trimmed away, exposing the backing sheet.

To add the surface of the path, carefully paint a narrow bead of diluted PVA along the trimmed-out groove using a narrow paintbrush. Then sprinkle Earth Powder, fine gravel or very fine scatter on top of the glue: when dry it creates a natural-looking surface (see Fig. 69).

Finely chopped fibres can be used to great effect along the edges of the path. In Fig. 70, such fibres have been carefully added to help blend the path's earth surface with the grasses that run alongside it. The fibres can be worked into position with a cock-tail stick, and are held in place with hairspray. Note how the edge of the backing sheet has been hidden by blending it into the groundwork using the finely chopped fibres.

The completed field can be enhanced even more with the addition of weeds and other scenic materials.

The close-up image of Raw Grass fibres in Fig. 72 shows just how finely they can be chopped. These particular fibres were coloured on the sheet before they were trimmed off and cut into the tiny lengths shown here.

As well as being useful for blending the edges of the fabric sheet into the surrounding groundwork, very finely chopped fibres are also most effective when used as moss. Fig. 73 shows a thin length of timber,

Fig. 69: *The path can be highlighted by using other materials.*

Fig. 70: *Blending the edges of a path into the grass that runs alongside it will improve its natural appearance.*

Fig. 71: *This image of the fur fabric field shows all the detail that can be created using a simple material.*

Fig. 72: *Very finely chopped Raw Grass fibres. These have been coloured using poster paint.*

which may have originated from an old barn or farm building, for example. Here it has been painted and weathered to represent old damp wood. A thin layer of PVA has been applied to the top of the beam, and whilst the glue was still wet, the fibres were placed on to the glue. As on the path edges above, they are best gently pushed into the glue using a cocktail stick or something similar, then given a light coat of hairspray, which will help them stay fixed in place. This technique is just as effective when used on rocks and so on.

Fig. 73: *Finely chopped Raw Grass fibres glued to wooden beams, rocks or tree trunks make very effective moss.*

Summary

Fur fabric is a very useful material for creating grass in a range of lengths. A sharp pair of scissors is all that is required to trim it, although good quality electric clippers can be used to good effect. The fabric is also versatile insofar as it can be easily coloured to suit a particular environment, and it is easily fixed to the layout with glue. It is also useful for tufts, blending groundwork together, and moss effects.

The three short-grass effects shown in this chapter can be used in conjunction with each other. Static grass can be applied to a bed of fine scatter, fur fabric tufts can be added to a field that mostly consists of static grass, and scatters can be fixed to both static grass fibres and fur fabric to replicate clumps of weeds and other ground-covering plants. The three materials are demonstrated together in the final section of this book.

Kevin Wilson's 'O' gauge 'Bucks Hill'. The beautiful sweeping curve of the track as it enters a tunnel mouth adds to the realism of the scene, as do the natural-looking contours of the terrain. The tall tree and dilapidated barn on top of the hill also add to the rural look of the landscape. Note the difference between the texture and colour of the grasses and ground cover on the railway side of the fence, and the grazed grass of the farmer's land. PAUL BAMBRICK

CHAPTER THREE

LONG GRASS EFFECTS

Fig. 74: Long grass growing in a field.

Certain grasses, when left to their own devices, can grow to a surprising height, easily three feet (90cm) or more. This demonstration involves the use of Raw Grass (teddy-bear fur fabric), which makes surprisingly realistic-looking long grass. The length of grass being modelled here is perfect for uncut fields, and for grass that grows around the perimeter of fields that have been cut or grazed. Raw Grass is also well suited for grasses that grow along walls and hedgerows. It can be easily coloured to suit the season in which your layout is set, and to suit its immediate surroundings within the layout.

Teddy-bear fur fabric, as shown in the previous demonstration for making short grass, is also very useful in the creation of long grass.

The fabric shown here is a small sheet of Raw Grass in its 'out of the box' appearance (see Fig. 75). The fibres on the sheet are approximately 25mm

Fig. 75: Uncoloured and untrimmed fur fabric in its natural state.

Fig. 76: The fibres on the sheet are brushed upright prior to colouring.

Fig. 77: The effect of the individual fibres can be seen here.

(1in) in height when stood upright, which equates to virtually six feet (two metres) high in 'OO' gauge (1:76 scale, or 4mm to the foot). When used as grass in 'OO' it is necessary to trim the fibres before colouring them. There are instances, even when modelling in 'OO', when the fibres can be left at the length they are, especially when the fabric is used as a frame for tall groups of weeds and nettles, which in nature can often reach six feet high. This technique will be demonstrated later on in the book.

If you are using Raw Grass for 'O' gauge (1:43 scale, or 7mm to the foot) or even larger scales, then it will produce very convincing tall grass without too much trimming at all. However, for 'O' gauge the fibres on the sheet do still benefit from a light trimming merely to add a slight variation to the length of the grass in the field; untrimmed the fibres equate to approximately 3ft 6in (just over a metre) in length.

Before colouring the fibres, and depending on how the grass is to be used, it is advisable to trim them to their final length – that is, the length you want the grass to appear on your layout. That said, for this demonstration I am leaving the grass untrimmed, in order to give an indication of the results that can be achieved without trimming the fibres beforehand.

If you choose to colour your Raw Grass sheet before trimming the fibres, then once the paint has dried, small tufts can be pinched with a thumb and

forefinger and then trimmed from the backing sheet using sharp scissors. These tufts can be glued directly to the layout using neat PVA glue, creating tufts of grass like the tufts seen in the reference photographs in Chapter 1.

Take the sheet and place it on a flat surface. Using your hand or a comb, brush the fibres so they stand fairly upright (see Fig. 76). Using a comb and the combing action also separates the fibres and allows the paint to be more easily dispersed throughout the sheet.

Another method of getting the fibres to stand is to take hold of the sheet with the fibres lying flat and facing you, and then flick the sheet using a whipping action. This will cause the fibres to stand upright.

The fibres on the sheet stand up fairly well even before they are painted (see Fig. 77), but the addition of paint helps the fibres to hold their upright position even better. When the grass is in position on your layout it can be given a spray of hairspray, which will hold the fibres even more securely, with less chance of the grass falling flat.

Sap Green acrylic paint is ideal for painting the Raw Grass sheet, as is pre-mixed, opaque poster paint. When using acrylic paints the paint should be diluted with water – six parts water to one of paint is a good strength of tone. The dilution level of the paint does depend on the strength of colour you

Fig. 78: Watercolour paints are used to colour the fabric in this demonstration.

Fig. 79: The paint is initially applied by hand.

desire, and it is recommended to colour a test piece first of all, to see if you are happy with the tone before you begin painting the whole sheet.

Some pre-mixed poster paints can be used without any further dilution, but again it may be prudent to test a small piece before starting work on a large area, as paint pigments will vary from different manufacturers. It is better to be in a position where more colour needs to be added, than where paint must be removed from the sheet (see Fig. 78).

When working with poster paints, apply the paint directly to your hand (see Fig. 79); the use of a rubber glove is optional, but not necessary at all. When working with acrylic paint, however, I would suggest dripping randomly spaced, diluted drops directly on to the sheet. Then rub the drops into the fibres by hand, using exactly the same technique as applying the pre-mixed poster paint, as shown in the photo.

Smear the paint lightly over the fibres: this will result in a fairly uniform covering over the sheet. Apply the paint against the nap of the fabric first – that is, pushing the fibres away from their original flat position, as can be seen on the fibres towards the back of the sheet. Then flatten the fibres with your hand so they lie down flat, as can be seen towards the front of the sheet (see Fig. 80). Add more paint to your hand as required.

Small amounts of watercolour paint may be added to vary the tones present in the grass. There are no strict rules when applying these highlight colours: they can be added using acrylic paints, poster paints, watercolours, even a small amount of oil-based paints, or they can be omitted altogether. Just a tiny amount of watercolour paint added with your fingertip will be enough to subtly enhance the grass.

Fig. 80: Work the paint through the fibres.

Fig. 81: Various tones of paint can be added, but it is important not to over-wet the fabric.

Fig. 82: Disperse the paint through the fibres using a comb or brush.

In Fig. 81 you will see that extra, yet small quantities of green poster paint have also been added to the fibres. It is important to note that the fabric is never actually wet with paint, nor should it ever be. Folding the fabric in half and rubbing it fibre to fibre is another good way of initially colouring the grass sheet.

Next, take an ordinary comb or brush and start to comb the fibres flat so they lie down in their original position – as they were when the sheet was

Fig. 83: Combing the paint through the fabric also helps to separate the fibres.

untouched. Combing not only flattens and separates the fibres, but is the best way to ensure that all the paint is dispersed throughout the sheet (see Fig. 82). You may need to be fairly heavy-handed with the comb in order to disperse the paint, but no damage will be done to the sheet. Expect some of the fibres to get stuck in the teeth of the comb and break away from the sheet. These fibres are useful later in the groundwork step, and ideally should be put aside for later use.

Remove any fibres you have picked up in the teeth of the comb. Hold the sheet down on a flat surface along the edge using your fingertips. Take the comb and brush the fibres in the opposite direction, forcing them to stand upright: this will help further disperse the paint throughout the sheet. It also helps separate the individual fibres on the sheet, as can be seen in Fig. 83. Note also the variation in the colour of the fibres, which becomes apparent as they are separated.

The sheet is once again combed flat so the paint is fairly evenly spread throughout the fibres (see Fig. 84). If at this stage the sheet appears to be overly wet, take a sheet of newspaper or a cloth and gently place it over the top of the sheet, then apply a little pressure so the excess paint is absorbed. Be careful not to remove too much paint, though, otherwise

Fig. 84: If the fabric is too wet, use a sheet of newspaper to blot up some of the paint.

Fig. 85: Finally comb the fibres so they stand upright and separated, allowing the paint to dry.

it may be necessary to add more by repeating the above procedures.

Finally take your comb or brush and comb the sheet so the fibres stand upright once more, thus allowing the paint to dry more easily (see Fig. 85).

The painting steps have been completed now, and what you have before you is a realistic-looking representation of long grass. As the paint dries, continue to comb the sheet, separating the fibres each time you comb. The realistic colour variation of the grass can be seen here.

Fig. 86 shows a close-up of the Raw Grass sheet after it has dried and with all the fibres separated. The colour of the grass will depend on the type of paint you use to colour it, and the amount of water you add to it when diluting it. Note that the individual fibres are not completely covered in paint, allowing some of the original colour of the fabric to show through. The use of yellow watercolour paint has given this area a yellower appearance.

Compare the coloured sheet of grass (see Fig. 86) with the grass on the hillside, which borders part of the East Lancs Railway (see Fig. 87). The similarity in both colour and texture is very apparent. For larger scales the sheet can be simply glued to the baseboard to represent a field or an overgrown embankment. For smaller scales the fibres can be

trimmed from the sheet using sharp scissors and glued in clumps to represent the longer grasses in this image. When used as tufts in this way this fabric will further enhance the appearance of the short-grass fields demonstrated in the previous chapter.

This close-up photograph shows that by colouring the fabric marginally darker, a completely different style of grass can be modelled (see Fig. 88). This time

Fig. 86: Note how the fibres are not a monotone colour, adding to the realism of the grass.

Fig. 87: Long grass growing along the track at Irwell Vale.

Fig. 88: Colour the grass to match your field trip photographs.

the fibres look lusher and more suited to a healthy meadow scene. Note that there are still variations in the colour of the fibres although they have a thicker coat of paint applied to them.

The colour of the Raw Grass in Fig. 88 is much more suitable if this is the style of grassy field being portrayed. For smaller scales, tufts of fibres can be trimmed from the sheet and used to represent the thick, dark green tufts apparent in this photograph (see Fig. 89). Trimming the sheet before colouring it gives you the option to leave longer tufts across the surface of the field, which can be highlighted by dry-brushing after the sheet has had a general coat of paint.

Paths and worn areas in the field are easily added to the fabric, either before or after it has been glued

Fig. 89: Long tufts of grass growing in a field.

Fig. 90: With care, all manner of grass effects can be achieved from a single sheet of fabric.

down. To create a path like the one shown in Fig. 90, simply trim away some of the long grass fibres, almost down to the backing fabric, using scissors. Apply diluted PVA glue to the path, and sprinkle on a suitable-coloured Earth Powder or scatter. A liberal spray of hairspray will help to fix the path surface. Note also the realistic variety of colours and textures visible in the field.

Fig. 91 shows a real path running through a real field. Note the way it meanders through the field, taking the easiest route over the uneven terrain; it is worn this way because people will generally take the course involving the least effort – which is something worth noting when adding paths to your own layouts. The dead stalks of plants add some variation to the colour in the field and around the tree trunks.

Fig. 91: Note how much shorter the grass is along the edge of the path when compared to the rest of the field.

Fig. 92: Colouring the grass to match the backscene will help create realistic perspective within the layout.

The long grass shown in Fig. 92 has been coloured using acrylic paint to match the grass in the distance on the hillside shown on the backscene. Picking out colours from your backscene and introducing similar tones into the foreground of the layout will bring the two elements together, creating a realistic balance between the two, which in turn creates a realistic-looking perspective to the scene.

Summary

Raw Grass (teddy-bear fur fabric) is an extremely versatile material when used to create long grass. It is easy to trim to the desired length, straightforward to colour using a variety or blend of paints, and, most importantly, can be coloured to match grasses that will suit any individual requirement, from pale straw-coloured grass to thick, lush, dark green grass. As can be seen in the above demonstration, it is also very good for creating moss, and is a good choice for tufts and other scenic effects that can be easily added to your groundwork.

Fig. 93: An interesting section of track as it approaches a bridge; note the long grass on each side of it.

Andy York and BRM Magazine, 'Black Country Blues', 4mm scale. Although the viaduct is the main feature in this scene, the carefully created landscape below it blends it realistically into the field it spans. Long grasses and small shrubs are skilfully used to blend its base into the field; the same materials are used in the field itself, as well as running along the roadside. The colour and texture on the surface of the road are also of note. The road is not an overall flat colour and contains wear and tear marks as well as interesting features where maintenance work has been carried out. ANDY YORK AND BRM MAGAZINE

CHAPTER FOUR

AGRICULTURAL FIELDS

Fig. 94: A tractor provides a little splash of red amongst the general green of the scenery.

The appearance of fields used for growing crops varies enormously from one crop to another, and also throughout the growing season. Each field takes on a different colour and texture depending on the type of crop grown in it, and by capturing the essence of a specific type of field, realistic-looking fields can be added to our layouts.

PLOUGHED FIELDS

The main purpose of ploughing is to turn the soil over in order to bring nutrients to the surface of the field and to bury weeds and unwanted seeds. The colour of soil varies from region to region, so if you want to create an authentic-looking ploughed field suited to your chosen location, it is well worth either making a field trip there armed with a camera, or taking some good reference photographs from the internet and working from those. Traditionally ploughs were drawn by working animals, but now

they are more often drawn by tractors: this means that if fields are modelled 'whilst they are being ploughed' we can also introduce extra features such as horses, tractors and farmhands into the scene.

Note that around the perimeter or sometimes just at each end of a field that is ploughed a strip of ground is left unploughed: this is referred to as the 'headland', and is where the tractor and plough turn round before continuing across the field ploughing parallel to the furrows already made. Fields are sometimes vast, and more often than not only a small section of field is modelled on the layout.

Mark the position of the hedge that will border the field, and fix it in place either before or after the groundwork has been completed. The headland area can be fashioned in any of the ways described in the two previous chapters regarding creating short or long grasses; here a blend of scatters, static grass fibres and earth, held in place with diluted PVA, has been used to create a rough-looking texture to

Fig. 95: The headland around a ploughed field.

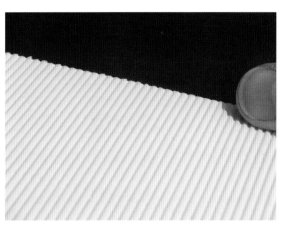

Fig. 96: A piece of corrugated card as a base for a
ploughed field is an ideal option.

the perimeter of the field (see Fig. 95). Note how
the bottom of the hedge has had glue, earth and
scatter added to it, which helps blend it into the
groundwork.

The surface of the ploughed field can be created in
a couple of ways. One method is to apply a thin layer
of plaster over the baseboard, and as it is drying drag
a specially made 'comb' over it, creating furrows in
the surface. However, it is far simpler to start off
with a material with a furrowed textured surface
such as a finely corrugated cardboard, and decorate
it accordingly; this is a 'tried and tested' method
which can result in a convincing ploughed surface
(see Fig. 96). Use a card with a corrugated pattern
that suits the scale you are working in.

The edge of the card that adjoins the headland
should be shaped with scissors so that it is not perfectly straight but makes a realistic join and fits into
the area of the field. Also, ploughed furrows are
rarely absolutely perfect, and the card benefits from
being squashed a little in places to look as if the soil
has fallen into the channels made by the blades of
the plough. The scissors can be used edge-on to
flatten some of the raised bits of card (see Fig. 97).
The furrows at the very edge of the card can be
flattened completely to help them blend into the
headland.

The card will benefit from an undercoat of paint,
ideally in a colour that roughly matches the eventual colour of the soil. Apply the paint either with a
brush or directly from an aerosol or airbrush, and
be sure to cover the card completely, especially if
it is white in colour, like the card being used in this
demonstration.

When the paint has dried, paint a thin coating of
PVA glue over the card, using a soft brush, making

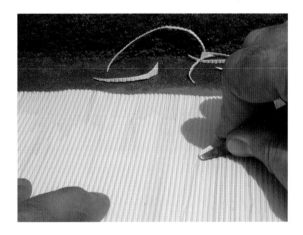

Fig. 97: Flattening some of the card adds detail to
the surface of the field.

Fig. 98: Apply a thin coat of neat PVA glue.

Fig. 99: Lightly cover the glue with an appropriately coloured scatter.

absolutely sure not to flood the grooves with glue (*see* Fig. 98).

Whilst the glue is still wet, sprinkle a fine layer of either Earth Powder or fine scatter over the glue. The scatter will add to the texture of the field, and will also add a more realistic coloration to the field (*see* Fig. 99).

When the surface of the field has dried it can be fixed to the baseboard. Paint a thin layer of PVA, or similar, on to the baseboard and sit the ploughed surface on it. Carefully push the card into the glue to help it stick (*see* Fig. 100). You can create a slight undulation in the surface of the field by placing a cocktail stick, matchstick or sliver of card underneath the card surface.

An interesting feature can be created by modelling a part of the field as yet unploughed. To achieve this, cover a small section of the field with static grass: neat PVA glue is painted on to the baseboard using a paintbrush, and the fibres applied using the

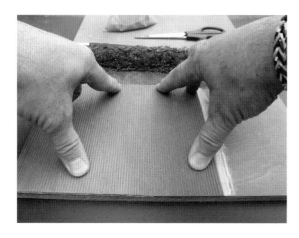

Fig. 100: Glue the card to the baseboard with its edge butted up to the headland.

Fig. 101: Tufts and scatter added to the unploughed section of the field.

Fig. 102: Carefully blend the edge of the card into the groundwork.

applicator. Then clear small areas of fibres, and sprinkle a little Earth Powder over them to resemble bare patches of soil. Here, small tufts have been created by dipping mixed static grass fibres into neat PVA, and these have been added to the bare patches. A little scatter completes the effect: this is sprinkled over the surface of the earth and pressed into the glue beneath (see Fig. 101).

All that remains is to blend the edge of the card into the headland. Here (see Fig. 102) a bead of diluted PVA has been painted round the perimeter of the card. Earth Powder and finely chopped Raw Grass fibres are worked into the glue, effectively blending the ploughed area of the field into the headland.

FEATURES IN AGRICULTURAL FIELDS

Even during the summer months puddles can often be seen in the fields of Great Britain, as can huge piles of manure in various stages of decay, waiting to be spread over the field surface; grasses have often started to grow on these manure heaps, and all these different features can add interest to the fields on our layouts (see Fig. 103).

Agricultural fields occasionally have permanent features in them, and the plough and crops must work round these, creating 'islands'. These may be where trees are growing, where a pylon is positioned or where there is a natural pond, for example, and modelling features such as these can add further interest to an otherwise fairly flat crop field. Sometimes these islands are fenced off from

Fig. 103: Puddles, mud and manure are all features that may be found in agricultural fields.

Fig. 104: Apply glue to the base of the mound and fix it to the baseboard.

Fig. 105: Static grass is applied using a Gras-master applicator.

the rest of the field, and the vegetation is generally left to grow wild.

To create a small island with, say, an ancient tree, take a small piece of material such as compressed paper ceiling tile, or polystyrene or Kingspan, and fashion it into a suitably sized and shaped mound; ensure that it is large enough to hold the feature that is to be placed on it. Apply glue to the underside of the mound, and fix it in position in the field (see Fig. 104). Note that the baseboard has already had a coat of a light brown matt emulsion paint, which acts as an undercoat for the scenic materials.

Short static grass fibres are used to create a young crop growing around the mound. The fibres are applied using an applicator, which charges them as they leave the hopper, ensuring they land in the glue vertically.

First, screw a metal hook, or hammer a nail into the baseboard in the area where you are adding the fibres. Using a paintbrush, apply a coat of static grass glue or PVA to the baseboard, adding it right up to the hook or nail; it is best to work on small areas at a time when adding the glue and fibres. Take the crocodile clip attached to your applicator and clip it to the hook. Fill the hopper with the chosen fibres and, following the instructions supplied with the applicator, cover the field right up to the edge of the mound (see Fig. 105).

An old tree with gnarled roots will be added to the top of the mound, but first the ceiling tile is carved out a little with a blade so the roots sit naturally on the surface of the ground (see Fig. 106).

The perimeter of the mound is fenced off from the rest of the field with rustic posts. To make the posts, use a sharp blade to trim cocktail sticks (for 'OO') or wooden skewers (for 'O') to roughly 20mm lengths, or longer depending on the scale you are working in; paint and weather them accordingly. Fix the posts round the perimeter of the mound, spacing them with approximately 25mm (1in) gaps or larger to suit; hold them secure with a spot of superglue or PVA. There is no need to fix them perfectly upright as the slight wonkiness of the posts will add to the charm of the feature. Wait for the glue to dry, then use a vacuum to remove any loose fibres or other unwanted debris from the field.

Apply a coat of PVA to the mound and add Earth Powder, short static grass fibres, finely chopped Raw Grass and scatter to the glue, thus creating an interesting-looking surface; longer tufts can then be glued on to the surface. Tufts and longer grass have been added to the edges of the mound; these are made using Raw Grass and long static grass fibres,

Fig. 106: Fence posts are fixed into the mound. Some of the tile is carved away to allow tree roots to fit snugly into the surface.

Fig 107: Build the scenic detail on the mound using various colours and textures.

and are intended to mask some of the fence posts, leaving only parts of them showing (see Fig. 107). Hold them in place using a spot of neat PVA, pressing them down into the groundwork using a cocktail stick.

In contrast to the greenery of the general scene, small clumps of fibres topped with colourful scatter are added to the mound, mostly with yellow and white flowers, but there is also a tiny clump with red flowers which adds further to the detail (see Fig. 108). It is the little eye-catching details that make even small features on our layouts stand out.

The finished island complete with an ancient tree makes an interesting feature in the field (see Fig. 109). The tree is held in place with a couple of spots of superglue, and its roots are blended into the mound using scatter and Earth Powder. The same techniques used for the island demonstrated here can be applied to small islands at the junctions of roads, whilst the techniques and methods required

Fig. 108: Colourful flowers add to the effect of the scenery.

Fig. 109: A dead tree completes the island.

Fig. 110: Rapeseed crop field in flower.

for creating trees like the one used in this demonstration are shown in detail in later chapters.

RAPESEED

In the nineteenth century rapeseed oil was produced as a source of lubricant for steam engines, but due to its bitter taste was less used for consumption. Today, rapeseed can be seen growing abundantly in fields all over Britain, as it has been cross-bred to produce a far more palatable oil, which is used in the food industry. Rapeseed fields are very easy to create and can add a mass of colour to our layouts. Rapeseed can grow up to five feet high (that is, 20mm/¾in in 'OO', and 35mm/1.3in in 'O').

To create a realistic-looking rapeseed crop in flower, the stalks and general greenery of the plant need to be modelled first. Although the yellow flowers do create a very thick blanket of colour, it adds to the realism of the field if the plant stems can be seen beneath the flower heads.

In this demonstration the stems of the plants are made using the fibres of a Raw Grass sheet. Static grass can also be used to create the long stems of the plant.

Take a sheet of Raw Grass fabric and cut it to fit the size and shape of the field. Brush up the fibres using your hand or a hairbrush or comb so they stand upright, and trim them to a suitable length if necessary; the fibres on this sheet are trimmed to approximately 15mm in height (see Fig. 111). Rapeseed fields are often surrounded by hedges, which hide the stems leaving only the flowering tops of the rapeseed showing, so it isn't always necessary to trim the fibres.

The fibres need to be painted green to represent the stalks; to do this, drip a few spots of water-based paint on to the sheet and rub them in by hand. The paint used for this field is Hooker's Green acrylic diluted in a ratio of four parts water to one of paint (see Fig. 112). Use a comb to work the paint through the fibres to disperse the paint. The material should never be overly wet, and will dry within half an hour. If you choose to spray an oil-based paint on to the fibres, avoid handling the sheet whilst the paint is wet as the fibres will stick together.

To add a little texture to the stems and give the appearance of green leaves growing on them, brush the fibres so they stand upright and spray the sheet with diluted PVA, hairspray, or matt varnish. Sprinkle

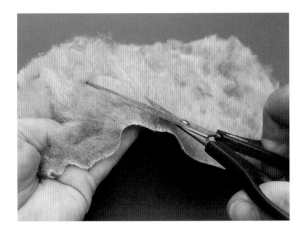

Fig. 111: Use sharp scissors to trim the fabric to length.

Fig. 112: Colour the 'stems' of the crop using diluted acrylic paint.

very fine green scatter among the fibres (see Fig. 113). When the sheet has dried it can be test fitted on the baseboard and any alterations then carried out.

To add the flower heads to the stems, take diluted PVA and spray it on to the fibres in the same way as for the green scatter (see Fig. 114). For small patches of rapeseed crop, PVA can be brushed on to the tips of the fibres.

Whilst the glue is still wet, take a bright yellow scatter and sprinkle it on to the wet glue. It is best to sprinkle on small amounts of scatter at a time, as more can easily be added to thicken up the density of the flowers.

Alternatively, if the sheet size allows it, it can be inverted and the tips of the fibres dipped into loose scatter spread on to a sheet of paper on a table top. If necessary use a wooden skewer to adjust the scatter

Fig. 113: Apply diluted PVA to the fibres, and sprinkle it over with a light coating of scatter.

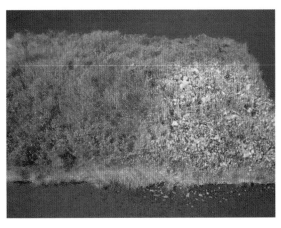

Fig. 114: Apply a further spray of diluted PVA to the fabric: this will hold the flowers in place.

Fig. 115: The scatter can be gently rearranged. Use a skewer to break up areas that appear too clumpy.

Wheat fields and other crops are easily created in a similar way using fur fabric; the fibres of the fabric are coloured to represent a particular crop. It is worth noting that wheat is green in appearance earlier in the growing season, turning to its more recognizable colour as it grows taller and ripens.

FALLOW AND OVERGROWN FIELDS

A 'fallow field' is a field that has been ploughed but left unplanted, with the aim of allowing the soil to regain its fertility for the next crop. Over the course of the season – or more than one season – these fields will be colonized by all manner of plants and weeds and will become wildly overgrown with an array of plants of varied colours and sizes.

The base of the field is given a coat of matt emulsion paint; here a grey/brown tone is used to represent a basic earth colour. This is to ensure that any small areas of board which are not covered in the process of adding the growth in the field show through as earth as opposed to bare wood colour. A sprinkling of Earth Powder is added to the paint to vary the colour and texture of the base layer (see Fig. 118).

in places where it appears to be too dense (see Fig. 115). Allow the glue to dry before adding the field to the layout. A thin coat of PVA glue applied to the baseboard will hold the sheet in place.

Fig. 116 shows the completed field bordered with a neatly trimmed hedge. The yellow-coloured flowers of the rapeseed make a striking contrast against the dark green foliage of the hedge.

Fig. 116: A rapeseed field will add a great deal of colour to layouts of any scale.

Fig. 117: Fallow or overgrown fields may contain all manner of grasses and plants.

The small patch of fallow field created in this demonstration contains long grasses, brambles, nettles and other weeds, forming a blanket of growth over the majority of the field. To make the clumps of long grasses that grow in the field, Raw Grass fabric is painted using diluted acrylic paints: follow the instructions in Chapter 3. When the fibres have dried, cut the sheet into random circular and oval shapes.

Take some of the smaller pieces of fabric and spray them with dilute PVA. Whilst the glue is still wet, sprinkle on fine scatter and short, bright green static grass fibres to create large clumps of weed growth. Dark scatter is very effective in making clumps that resemble nettles. Use different colours of scatter, or blends of scatter, on the various pieces of fabric to create a variety of tall-growing plants. Give the tips of the fibres a light covering of glue

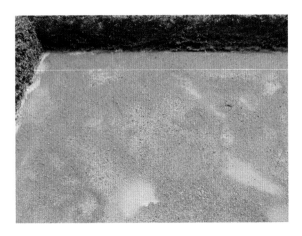

Fig. 118: Earth Powder is applied over the painted undercoat.

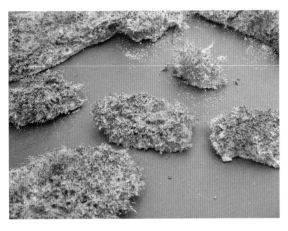

Fig. 119: Clumps of tall weeds are created; some can have flowers added to them.

Fig. 120: Hold the clumps in place using PVA glue, painted directly on to the baseboard. Push the materials down into the glue using a wooden skewer.

Fig. 121: Static grass fibres, earth and scatters are added to the groundwork.

with a paintbrush, and then sprinkle them with coloured scatter to represent flowers (see Fig. 119). The clumps can be put aside to dry, or can be fixed to the baseboard straight away.

It is advisable to test the clumps in different positions before fixing them permanently in place; this can be done either before adding the scatters to them, or once they have dried. To fix the clumps to the baseboard, apply some neat PVA to the baseboard using a paintbrush and carefully sit them in place. Use a thin wooden skewer to push the centre and edges of the clumps on to the board to ensure they come into contact with the glue (see Fig. 120).

Take some PVA and apply it in random spots to the surface of the board, then press some long static grass fibres into these. Coat the rest of the field with diluted PVA using a soft paintbrush, and sprinkle a mixture of fine and coarse scatters to add texture to the surface of the field; leave patches of the earth showing through, or leave a path through to the adjoining field. Add a light covering of short static grass fibres to any patches of glue that remain visible (see Fig. 121).

The edges of the Raw Grass clumps of weed can be blended into the groundwork at this stage. Take some coloured Raw Grass fibres and trim them, using sharp scissors, into tiny fibres. Then work these

fibres round the edge of the backing on clumps, again using a thin wooden skewer, which will ensure there is little disturbance to the rest of the groundwork.

To create brambles for the field, take a piece of rubberized horsehair and pull some of the fibres away from it. Shape the fibres into rounded mounds of stems, then paint them using an aerosol or airbrush. Bramble stems change colour over the growing season, changing from green to dark red, and if you want to indicate a particular time of year it is worth noting what colour they are then. The undersides of the mounds will benefit from a spray of black paint to indicate shade.

Spray the fibres with dilute PVA and sprinkle them with a scatter that represents the season you are modelling; a spray of hairspray will help the scatter stick. Place the mounds directly on to PVA glue applied to the surface of the field, and blend them into the groundwork using chopped fibres of Raw Grass (see Fig. 122).

Light-coloured tufts of grass growing amongst the other plants in the field add to the colours and textures. Trim small tufts from the sheet using scissors, and dip their bases into neat PVA or similar glue with a thick consistency. Place the tufts on to the field, making sure they come into contact with the baseboard. The base of each tuft can be blended into the

Fig. 122: Blend the weeds and brambles into the groundwork using finely chopped fibres.

Fig. 123: Individual tufts are held in place with PVA. A little Earth Powder helps blend them into the existing groundwork.

rest of the field with one of the materials already in use; here a little Earth Powder is sprinkled over the glue (*see* Fig. 123). Add as many single tufts and larger patches of fibres as required; use a cocktail stick to make the fibres stand more upright if necessary.

Next, a small sapling is positioned against the hedge among the general growth of the field. Saplings add height to the scene, and can be a feature of fallow and overgrown fields (*see* Fig. 124).

Ready-to-use tufts are a good choice of material for filling in some of the gaps between the various plants (*see* Fig. 125). Dip their bases into glue and position them accordingly.

Fig. 124: Saplings add a little extra height to the field.

Fig. 125: Ready-to-use tufts are useful for filling gaps in between the plants.

Fig. 126: Push the tufts into the groundwork.

Fig. 127: The completed scene.

To ensure the tufts stick to the scenery already in place, push them into the groundwork with the aid of a wooden skewer (see Fig. 126).

The photograph of the completed fallow field (see Fig. 127) shows some of the elements that may be found in such a field: generally there is more long grass evident, with the tufts, weeds and brambles spread out over a larger area than the demonstration field shown here. Note how all the differing colours and textures in the field harmonize to create a realistic-looking, balanced scene. A path meanders through the field and joins the rapeseed field behind it, continuing through the crop and out the other side.

Fig. 128: Young wheat crop; note the green colour.

FROM LEFT TO RIGHT:

Fig. 129: Wheat fields change in colour as they mature.

Fig. 130: A grass field cut and baled up for haylage.

Fig. 131: Young corn planted in neat rows.

Pendon Museum's EM-gauge 'Midland and South Western Junction Railway'. The Pendon Museum's model railway is truly a model of a railway running through a natural-looking landscape. Not only do the long, sweeping curves of the railway make this scene very realistic, but also the colours used in it, and the continuity of their use across the whole layout. The contrast between the dark foliage of the trees and the muted tones of the grass is of particular note. Note, too, the fence separating the railway and the farmland, allowing the cattle to roam freely. ANDY YORK AND BRM MAGAZINE

CHAPTER FIVE

TRIMMED HEDGES

Fig. 132: A neatly trimmed laurel hedge.

Materials

- Rubberized horsehair
- Aerosol paint – black/brown
- Hairspray
- Scatters
- Diluted PVA glue (three water/one glue)
- Wire
- Bark Powder

Tools

- Sharp scissors
- Wire cutters
- Atomizer bottle
- Paintbrush

NEATLY TRIMMED HEDGES

To create neatly trimmed hedges, take a block of rubberized horsehair and, holding it firmly in one hand, cut narrow strips from it using sharp scissors (see Fig. 133). The strips can be marked out on the block prior to cutting using a fine marker pen and a ruler, and these lines used as a guide when cutting. How wide you cut the strips depends on the scale you are working in: the sheets are usually about 25mm in thickness, therefore a hedge standing approximately 25mm high in 'OO' equates to a hedge in real terms standing six feet (2m) tall, while used for an 'O'-gauge layout it would represent a hedge standing approximately three and a half feet (1m) tall, which in reality would be a very low hedge indeed. And if it were being made for an 'N'-gauge layout it would stand approximately twelve feet (3.5m) tall, which is tall, but certainly not unheard of.

The hedge here represents a neatly trimmed six-foot (2m) hedge for use on a 'OO'-gauge model

Fig. 133: Trim rubberized horsehair into narrow strips using sharp scissors.

Fig. 134: Round the top of the hedge by trimming off the square edges.

railway. To create a symmetrical domed top to the hedge, take a pair of sharp scissors and carefully trim the 'square' edge away from both sides of the top of the hedge (see Fig. 134). Rubberized horsehair has a denser side and a more open side to the block: for neat hedges use the denser side at the top of the hedge. Even manicured hedges are often never faultless when it comes to their shape, so don't aim for perfection at this stage.

Trimming the bottom of the hedge into a narrow wedge will create a pleasing and realistic shape at the base: use scissors to do this. Again, the angle needn't be perfect all the way along the hedge, but just make sure the base is slightly narrower than the sides (see Fig. 135). Trimming also removes any long straggly fibres.

Rubberized horsehair is a flexible material and so can be used to produce long lengths of curving

Fig. 135: Make the base of the hedge slightly narrower than the sides, and remove any long fibres.

Fig. 136: Cocktail sticks make useful planting pins positioned along the base of the hedge.

hedging. To hold the hedging in place on the layout, small planting pins can be inserted and glued into the bottom of the hedge. Take several cocktail sticks and cut or snap them approximately in half. Give each stick a thin coat of dark brown or black paint, and dip it into neat PVA glue or superglue. Whilst the glue is still wet, insert the stick into the bottom of the hedge, leaving the pointed end sticking out from the base; allow the glue to dry (see Fig. 136).

Spray the hedge with a *light* coat of paint using a mid to dark brown or black — a mix of both works well (see Fig. 137). The paint can be sprayed directly from an aerosol can or applied using an airbrush. Optionally small amounts of green paint can also be sprayed on, to represent algae and moss, but this is usually unnecessary where foliage is being fixed to the hedge.

Spray the hedge with a liberal amount of hairspray (see Fig. 138): the hairspray can be applied to the hedge whilst the paint is still wet, or you can let it dry first if you prefer.

Take small pinches of scatter and cover the hedge with an even sprinkling. Apply a heavier coating of scatter if you require a denser hedge, and a lighter covering if you want it to be more open and airier in appearance. A lighter covering will allow the structure of the hedge to show through (see Fig. 139).

Planting Pins

Small wooden planting pins are an ideal method to use when your hedge will be following the curves of a railway line, lane or road. Positioning the sticks at approximately 150mm (½in) intervals along the length of the hedge gives good control over the curves when fixing it to the layout. The cocktail sticks can be pushed into the soft terrain on the layout, or small holes can be drilled at 150mm intervals and the pins inserted into them. A spot of glue will help hold the pins into the board.

Of course the pins can be fixed to the baseboard first at closer intervals and painted to represent fence posts. Then the completed hedge can be placed over them, making a good representation of a hedge following the line of an older fence.

The very bottom of the hedge is purposely kept clear of scatter so that it appears less dense (see below).

The hedge will benefit visually from the addition of a very light sprinkling of a different-coloured scatter to its top and sides. Apply more hairspray to the hedge and use a fine scatter if possible, especially if it is brighter in colour than the first: this will give an impression of newer and fresher growth, which is

Fig. 137: Give the horsehair a light spray of paint: this will improve the look of the finished hedge.

Fig. 138: Spray the hedge with a liberal amount of hairspray.

Fig. 139: The first application of dark scatter is added. The density of the hedge is dictated by the amount of scatter that is added.

Fig. 140: Highlights are added using a lighter-coloured scatter.

especially effective when applied to hedges and trees that are being created for a spring or early summer layout (see Fig. 140).

Once you are happy with the distribution and thickness of the scatter, take your diluted PVA and give the whole hedge a good misting using the atomizer. It is a feature of hedges to sometimes have a thicker and more concentrated covering of foliage in certain areas along their length than in others. This effect can be easily created by applying the scatter more thickly in some places than in others. If the spraying action of the glue displaces too much scatter, more can be applied to the hedge whilst the PVA is still wet. A liberal spray of hairspray will help the glue soak into the scatter on the hedge ensuring it adheres to the rubberized horsehair.

The hedge at this point will be very wet, and it is advisable to allow it to dry before planting it on the layout. Note that the very bottom of the hedge is purposely kept clear of scatter so that it appears less dense, a feature that can often be observed in natural hedges (see Fig. 141).

Holes for the planting pins can be marked and drilled either before adding the scatter to the hedge, or once the hedge is completely dry. Either use a narrow drill bit to drill neat holes vertically into the board, or if you have used a soft material to shape the terrain, simply push the cocktail sticks into the

Fig. 141: The finished hedge ready for planting.

Fig. 142: A little PVA painted along the bottom of the hedge will hold it securely in place.

surface. If necessary add a little glue into each hole – PVA or superglue is ideal. You can also apply a little neat PVA glue along the bottom of the hedge to help keep it in position (see Fig. 142).

FRESHLY FLAILED HEDGES

Hedges growing in parks and gardens and along railway lines, road sides and on open farmland all need trimming to keep them in a healthy state and to ensure they remain dense and do not start encroaching on to the places they border. Hedges modelled in a way that suggests they have recently been trimmed or indeed are in the process of being trimmed are easy to create, and enable us to introduce 'work in progress' scenes to our layouts.

This demonstration shows how to create the look of a hedge that is in the process of being trimmed. The materials used are a mix of rubberized horsehair and canopy material. This style of hedge can actually be made in two or more sections which are joined together once they are added to the landscape; however, this demonstration concentrates on the area where the two styles join, and the hedge is made as one component.

Take a block of rubberized horsehair and trim off a length using sharp scissors. Plenty of hedges that are trimmed back hard from time to time are as wide as they are tall, so this strip is about 25mm (1in) in width as well as in height (see Fig. 144).

Decide on the point where you would like the hedge to change from its trimmed appearance to a more natural and overgrown state. Using your fingers, start to pull and tease open the fibres on the overgrown side (see Fig. 145): this section can be pulled and shaped as much as you want to develop the width and height of the hedge to suit your specific requirements. Also pull apart and separate the fibres of a separate piece of rubberized horsehair: these will be cut off and used to represent the freshly trimmed growth lying on the ground along the length of the trimmed part of the hedge.

To add even more textural difference to the hedge, take a plait of Canopy material and tease some of the fibres from it. Pull them so they are open in structure, and carefully place them on the overgrown section of the hedge (see Fig. 146). There is no need to apply glue to the fibres at this stage as the paint and glue used later in their construction will hold all the various elements of the hedge together.

Fig. 143: A well-trimmed hedge joins a more overgrown section.

Fig. 144: A 25mm (1in) square length of rubberized horsehair.

Fig. 145: Tease out the fibres of the overgrown section.

Take a dark brown or black aerosol and apply a light coat of paint to both the hedge and the pile of loose cut rubberized horsehair fibres (see Fig. 147). The paint makes the skeleton of the hedge a better colour, and also helps to strengthen the delicate canopy fibres. Allow it to dry before continuing with the next step.

Take sharp scissors and carefully trim the neat section of the hedge; most hedges are trimmed into a flat-topped 'A' shape (see Fig. 148). Trimming with scissors not only refines the shape of the hedge, it also highlights where the fibres are cut, because the original and natural colour of their tips then stands out against the paint covering. The trimmed ends of the 'branches' can be highlighted even more if they are dry-brushed with a 'wood'-coloured paint.

All that remains is to apply scatter to the overgrown hedge to represent foliage; choose a scatter

Fig. 146: Synthetic hair fibres are added over the teased-out rubberized horsehair.

Fig. 147: A light spray of paint helps to blend the two kinds of fibre together, and strengthens the canopy.

Fig. 148: The trimmed section has been shaped into a flat-topped, 'A'-shaped hedge.

Fig. 149: Small piles of freshly cut hedge are prepared and will be added to the groundwork around the hedge once it is on the layout.

or mix of scatters suited to your chosen season. Take an aerosol of hairspray and apply a misting to the hedge. A tiny amount of scatter can also be applied to the trimmed side of the hedge, to create the look of foliage that hasn't been removed, or which has started to grow back after a recent trim; in this example the hedge has been freshly cut, so only a little scatter will be added to the neat section. Spray the trimmings as well as the hedge, and sprinkle these with scatter too.

Make up some small piles of the trimmed fibres: these will be placed on the ground along the length of the trimmed section of hedge (see Fig. 149). Spray both the hedge and the piles with diluted PVA to hold all the materials together; a spray of hairspray will also help strengthen the features. Keep aside a few loose trimmings, which can be scattered randomly on the ground around the scene.

The hedge should be fixed to the groundwork using glue, or pins and glue as with the trimmed hedge demonstrated previously, and worked into the surrounding groundwork using the methods shown at the end of the chapter.

When the piles of trimmings are added to the front of the trimmed length of hedge the result is very convincing and tells the story of the work being done (see Fig. 150). This method of creating

hedges can also be used where two hedges meet at the border of two fields, giving the impression that one is better maintained than the other. The field behind the trimmed hedge could be ploughed or have crops growing in it, whilst the overgrown hedge may enclose a fallow field. The hedge between the two fields could be trimmed on one side and overgrown on the other.

Fig. 150: The two styles of hedge are well illustrated here.

NARROW HEDGES FOR AUTUMN OR WINTER

This demonstration shows how to create realistic open hedging for autumn and winter scenes; this style of hedge can also have leaves applied, but will look best with only a very light covering as some of the detail will be lost underneath the scatter.

WORKING WITH WIRE

The style of hedge being demonstrated here is an introduction to modelling scenic features with wire. The methods and techniques shown combine the hedge-making materials demonstrated previously with some of the techniques and materials you will use when creating larger hedgerow shrubs, bushes and trees. This style of hedging can be created for most scales but is best for 'OO', 'O' and larger scales. Fine wire is an extremely functional material when used in the making of scale model scenery; its use in relation to trees is demonstrated in detail later in the book.

Select some single wires: here, 0.7mm wires are used. Cut them into 50–60mm (2–2½in) lengths, and tap one end of the wires on a hard surface to make a flat end; the wires are collected into bundles containing approximately twelve wires each. Take one of the wires from a bundle and start winding it round the rest of the wires to create a small 'trunk'. When you are part way up, bend a few of the wires to one side, creating a small side branch; twist these wires together, then divide them into two creating more side branches. Continue winding and separating until all the wires you bent to one side have been used. Take another wire and start winding it around the trunk, creating more short side branches as you proceed.

When all the wires have been used, hold the base of the 'tree' in one hand, and with the other, pull the side branches so they are all facing almost upright, creating a rather flat structure. These mini trees are the framework for the hedge so you will need to make a batch of them, allowing for at least one every scale six feet – that is, approximately twelve to thirteen for 'OO' gauge, and seven to eight for 'O', for each foot of hedge created. The lower part of the trunks can be covered with a thin layer of masking tape to hide the wires winding round them (see Fig. 152).

Take some Bark Powder or plaster and mix it with a little diluted PVA glue to form a paste that is runny enough to apply with a fine paintbrush. Apply the bark with the brush, covering the wires as you

Fig. 151: A length of narrow, open-structured hedge as it appears in winter.

Fig. 152: Small wire armatures are constructed for the framework of the hedge.

Fig. 153: Cover the armatures with bark; alternatively they can simply be painted.

proceed (see Fig. 153). When the bark has dried the structures can be painted and weathered to give the appearance of old, well flailed hedging plants; alternatively they can simply be painted and weathered without the addition of bark. Put them to one side to allow the paint to dry.

Take the block of rubberized horsehair and with sharp scissors, trim thin strips from it. The thickness of these strips is approximately 10–12mm at the top. Note how the top of the block is manufactured very flat: a hedge that has been kept to a certain height over a long period of time would look like this. The lower parts of the hedge can be thinned out even more to produce a very open structure (see Fig. 154). This length of hedging has been lightly sprayed with black paint and then given a light spray of mid-brown paint from above; this creates a realistic impression of shade within the hedge.

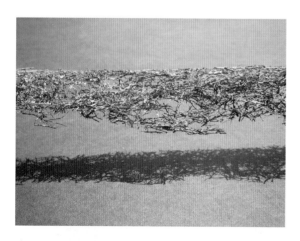

Fig. 154: Trim a very thin length of rubberized horsehair and lightly spray with paint.

Fig. 155: Insert the wire armatures into the rubberized horsehair, holding them in place using superglue.

Work the wire armatures into the horsehair, making sure the wires reach into the hedge, and fix them in place using a little superglue; it may be necessary to trim off the single wires to make it easier to push the armatures into the horsehair. Position them along the length of the hedge; here they are placed at approximately scale six-feet intervals (*see* Fig. 155). This step can be a little fiddly, but the result is well worth the care and effort. Note that up to half the length of the 'trunks' of these armatures is used to plant the hedge into the baseboard, bringing the bottom of the hedge closer to the groundwork. Optionally a little green paint dry-brushed or sprayed on to the hedge will help 'weather' it if required.

APPLYING THE FOLIAGE

As explained above, this demonstration shows how to create realistic open hedging for autumn and winter scenes. This style of hedge can also have leaves applied, but will look best with only a very light covering as some of the detail will be lost underneath the scatter representing foliage. To apply the scatter, spray the hedge with hairspray, then lightly sprinkle it over with a fine scatter. Finally seal the hedge using dilute PVA applied with an atomizer and a secondary coat of hairspray.

Fig. 156: Small holes in the baseboard will hold the hedge in place.

To fix the hedge to the layout, drill small holes into the baseboard that correspond to the positions of the armatures in the hedge, and insert the ends of the wire, fixing them with glue if necessary. Alternatively, if the materials used on the layout are soft enough, make small holes in the surface of the terrain and push the armatures into them. This section of hedge has been fixed into a length of Kingspan (*see* Fig. 156).

Fig. 157: Long grasses and weeds tend to grow along the base of hedges in the wild.

Using a wide paintbrush, apply a generous amount of diluted PVA along the front of the hedge, making sure the glue reaches right to the base of the hedge. On hedges that reach the ground, paint some of the glue on to the bottom of the hedge too, as the bottoms of hedges can often adopt the colour of the ground around them due to the action of the wind and rain, much as trains do as they travel through the landscape (see Figs 158 & 159).

Take small pinches of either Earth Powder or very fine earth-coloured scatter, and sprinkle it over the wet glue, allowing some of it to cover the glue on the hedge, too. You will see the glue being soaked up by the Earth Powder (see Fig. 160).

Add a few more drops of glue in random areas along the base of the hedge and sprinkle small pinches of scatter to represent low-growing plants, moss and even ivy growing at the foot of the hedge. If you use a dark 'ivy'-coloured scatter it can be effective to add some growing up the wire armatures, too. This can easily be applied by adding a small amount of either neat or diluted PVA to the armatures and carefully applying the 'ivy' to it (see Fig. 161).

For the rest of the scatters along the hedge use a variety of colours making sure they are the same as, or at least complement, the rest of the colours used, or are reserved for the rest of the scenic work on the layout; a pinch of static grass fibres is also

Blending Hedges into the Landscape

Hedges can be 'planted' into the scenery on the layout after the fields, lanes or roads that they line have been created, or they can be added to the layout before the rest of the scenic work, and blended into the groundwork as the materials around them are introduced to the baseboard.

Whichever sequence you choose, a certain amount of blending in will be required to ensure the hedges on your layout look as if they are growing from the ground amongst all the other grasses and plants, as opposed to just sitting on the surface. Of course, hedges in parks and along roads are sometimes kept clear of growth around them, and look the part simply growing from a bed of earth or gravel. This demonstration, however, assumes the hedge is in a more natural setting, growing at the side of a lane.

added at this stage, to ensure the whole scene blends together and looks natural.

Long grass and tufts of grass and weeds can often be seen growing along the fronts of hedges. For the general growth along the hedge, Raw Grass fibres are worked into the groundwork held in place with PVA.

Fig. 158: Note how the bottom of this hedge is weathered by the surrounding soil.

Fig. 159: Apply dilute PVA around the base of the hedge.

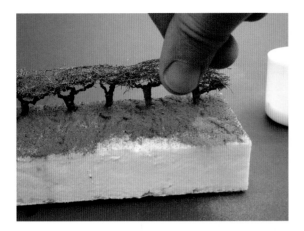

Fig. 160: Earth Powder is sprinkled on the wet glue.

Fig. 161: Fine scatters and static grass fibres are added along the base of the hedge.

Use fibres that have been coloured in slightly different tones of green and yellowy green to add some variation to the hedge (see Fig. 162). A misting of hairspray will hold all the elements of the hedge in place.

Small flowers are an eye-catching feature sometimes associated with the ground around hedges – even the smallest addition of colour, even if not instantly apparent, will add to the overall appearance of the groundwork. Using colours that are evident elsewhere on the layout or in the immediate area around the hedge will bring all the elements of the scene together in harmony.

Fig. 162: Long grasses and weeds complete the hedge, blending it in with its surroundings.

Fig. 163: A wide variety of hedges border this country lane.

SUMMARY

Hedges are an incredibly common and important feature of the British landscape, and can be worked into most model railway layouts, be they based on rural locations or set in a more urban landscape. The hedges demonstrated here range from the very simple and easy to produce to those that require a little more planning and skill; none of them, however, are particularly difficult to make, and they are an attractive feature that will enhance your layout.

When you are out on your field trips note how tall some hedges can actually be, and how neatly cut some are, even in farmland areas.

Fig. 164: A tiny leaf adds extra detail to the top of this hedge.

Fig. 165: Wildflowers add a splash of colour along the front of this hawthorn hedge.

Fig. 166: A well-trimmed rubberized horsehair hedge with 'fresh growth' on top.

CHAPTER SIX

MIXED HEDGES

Fig. 167: A huge variety of plants and bushes make up the hedges bordering this lane.

Garden and park hedges are often planted using only one species of plant – privet, laurel or beech for instance – and are generally tended on a regular basis, keeping them neat in appearance and free from other invasive plants. Hedges growing along country lanes can show a greater degree of both colour and texture variation due to the assortment of plants growing within them. Young saplings can also take root along these hedgerows.

Take a block of rubberized horsehair and trim 15–25mm (½–1in) wide strips from it, wider if you are modelling in a large scale. The exact width of the strips isn't very important as they will be teased and pulled apart. To do this, take hold of the strip in one hand, and with the other pull the fibres to form an open structure. These strips are very easy to join together seamlessly at the ends when fixing them to the layout: simply push them together. You will find it easier for constructional purposes to work with 30–45cm (12–18in) lengths, which are easy to handle; join them together later on the layout. Note

how the flatter side of the rubberized horsehair is used as the base of the hedge (see Fig. 168).

Using scissors, trim off the long fibres and remove them from the hedge; also trim small sections from

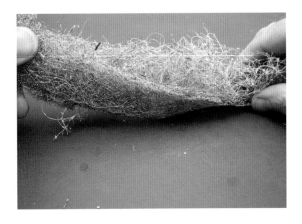

Fig. 168: Use the flatter side of the rubberized horsehair as the base for this hedge.

Fig. 169: Scissors are used to shape the upper part of the hedge; the fibres have been teased apart to form an airy structure.

Fig. 170: Colour the rubberized horsehair with different shades of aerosol paint, the darkest first, the lightest last.

the top of the hedge to give some variation in height along its length (*see* Fig. 169).

Take an aerosol or airbrush and spray the horsehair with a light coat of paint, using mid brown, dark brown or black; an application of all three colours will add some extra depth to the look of the hedge, but is not an essential part of its construction. If you choose to use more than one paint to spray your hedges, use the darkest first to create shade within

the hedge, then apply the lighter tones to the outer 'branches' (*see* Fig. 170).

Spray the horsehair with hairspray and apply a layer of scatter to the whole length of the hedge (*see* Fig. 171). The more scatter you add at this stage, the denser the hedge will appear. A hedge is usually more open in structure in some places than others, and it can add interest to your overall landscape if you represent some parts of it as being less bushy than others.

Fig. 171: Sprinkle a basic green-coloured scatter over the whole hedge.

Fig. 172: An addition to the hedge is a finer synthetic hair covered in a lighter green scatter.

Fig. 173: Carefully work the synthetic hair into the rubberized horsehair using a wooden skewer.

Fig. 174: Spray the whole structure liberally with diluted PVA; allow to dry.

To add contrast to both the colour and texture of the foliage of the hedge, tease out small pinches of canopy material – finer synthetic hair – spray them with aerosol paint and then hairspray, and sprinkle them with a lighter tone of green scatter (see Fig. 172). These are made in exactly the same way as small, low-growing bushes used to build up ground cover. When the scatter is in place, apply another layer of hairspray.

Using scissors, trim small clumps off the lighter green canopy hair and carefully place them on top of the rubberized horsehair, working them into the hedge with a thin wooden skewer (see Fig. 173). Let the fine hair sit on top of the hedge to represent newer, brighter growth.

When the canopy has been worked into the hedge, spray the whole hedge with diluted PVA in a ratio of three parts water to one PVA (see Fig. 174); extra scatter can be added to the wet glue at this stage if necessary, and topped off with a further spray of hairspray. The hedge should then be allowed to dry. Once it is dry the scatter will be fixed firmly in place, making handling much easier.

Detail can be added using Seamoss. Take a piece of Seamoss and apply a light coat of paint to it using an airbrush or aerosol. The piece in Fig. 175 has been sprayed very lightly with a matt, mid-brown-coloured paint. Once the paint has dried, cut the small side branches away from the main stalk and dip the very tips into diluted PVA glue. Sprinkle scatter over the glue creating an open branch structure (see Fig. 175). Note how a couple of small pieces of Seamoss have been sprayed a lighter shade to resemble dead branches.

Dip the end of the Seamoss stalk into neat PVA glue and push the stem of the cutting into the top of the hedge. These pieces look at their best when applied as if growing proud of the top of the hedge

Fig. 175: Paint small pieces of Seamoss and attach scatter to their tips.

Fig. 176: Fix the pieces of Seamoss to the hedge with superglue so they look as if they are growing through and above it.

Fig. 177: Small pieces of rubberized horsehair covered with dark scatter are added to the front of the hedge.

(see Fig. 176); trim them with scissors to neaten them if necessary. Note how the difference in colour between the black paint used on the hedge and the brown paints used on the Seamoss add to the natural appearance of the hedge.

To add the impression of ivy growing in the hedge, take a small piece of rubberized horsehair and chop the fibres into short lengths, arranging them to make a fairly flat structure. Spray them with paint and then hairspray, and add some dark green scatter highlighted with a lighter green scatter; then seal with a spray of diluted PVA. The ivy is best worked into the hedge once it has dried; it can be fixed to the front of the hedge using superglue or PVA (see Fig. 177).

Fig. 178: Hedges, hedgerows and rows of trees can be surprisingly tall. Compare the trees behind the track to the height of the loco.

MAKING SAPLINGS AND YOUNG TREES

Saplings, by their very nature, have slender branches and trunks so when making them use very fine wire. This demonstration uses wires with a 0.3mm diameter (approximately 1in in 'OO' and only about ½in in 'O').

MAKING SAPLINGS: FIRST METHOD

Cut the selected wires to the required length (see Fig. 179). Account for the 'trunk' of the sapling armature to be pushed right down into the hedge, and for the remainder to stick up through the top of the hedge.

Take up the wires, holding one end of them between your finger and thumb or a pair of pliers, gripping tightly; then with your other hand twist them together tightly to form a narrow trunk. The more tightly the wires are wound together, the more condensed the trunk will get, and then you may avoid having to add a coat of bark to the wires, which instead can be simply painted over, the pattern of the twisted wires creating the effect of bark texture. Bear in mind that trees sticking out of hedges will only require branches at the top of the trunk.

When the lower section of the trunk has been created and the wires are held together tightly, you can start making branches by bending wires away from the trunk. Bend two wires and twist them together to create a fork in the branch; then tighten the remaining wires of the trunk by twisting them using just your hand. Work a little way up, then make another branch by taking two more wires and bending them away from the trunk on the opposite side, creating another a fork. Repeat this step of twisting and selecting a side branch, though use single wires towards the top of the tree; continue until all the wires have been used up. The result is a very effective-looking small sapling armature (see Fig. 180).

In Fig. 181 the sapling has been given a coat of paint and made to look slightly weathered. A few spots of glue added to its trunk are enough to hold

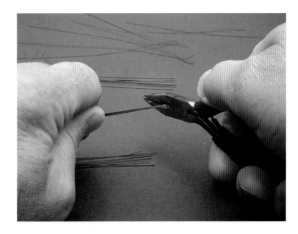

Fig. 179: Start making small saplings by cutting fine wires to the appropriate length.

Fig. 180: The completed sapling armature. It is not always necessary to cover the wires of saplings with bark; sometimes they can simply be painted.

it in place in the hedge. Push it down into the hedge until it is the height you require.

The foliage canopy for the sapling armature is created in the same way as the hedge growth made using the canopy material (see Fig. 182). The hair fibres are teased out and covered with scatter, which is held in place with hairspray and diluted PVA. A small amount of PVA is applied to the tips of the branches using a fine paintbrush, and the canopy is carefully placed on to the armature, making sure the fibres adhere to the glue. When dry the glue will not be seen.

Fig. 181: The sapling armature is painted and fixed into the hedge.

Fig. 182: A light and airy canopy is added to the armature.

MAKING SAPLINGS: SECOND METHOD

For the second method that can be used for creating saplings or very slender trees, proceed as follows. Take a few lengths of very fine wire and trim them to the approximate height you want your finished tree to be; if it is to be free-standing and not part of a hedge allow a little extra length, which can be inserted into the baseboard to hold the tree in position. Next, trim more fine wires into short lengths, for the branches of the tree.

Take the wires for the trunk and twist them together; separate the wires at the top of the trunk to form the crown of the tree.

Next, take one of the short wires you have trimmed for the branches and make a small loop in the centre of it. Thread the 'trunk' wire through the loop, and pull both ends of the side branches away from each other to tighten the loop around the trunk (see Fig. 183). A little spot of superglue will help hold the branches in place. This procedure may be repeated as many times as you want, creating

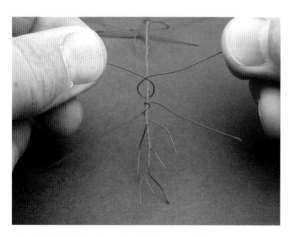

Fig. 183: Pull both ends of the wire tight, creating two side branches.

Fig. 184: Trim the branches to length and position them round the trunk. Bend them so they point upwards.

a series of side branches without thickening up the trunk, something which is especially useful when creating saplings.

Use your hands to bend the trunk and create a natural-looking sapling shape; use scissors or wire cutters to trim the branches to length, and position them accordingly. The branches of saplings often grow upwards at an angle of about 45 degrees (see Fig. 184).

If you choose to add bark to the wires, allow it to dry and then give it a wash of paint. Young saplings usually need only a suitably coloured wash of paint, and do not require much weathering effect. Saplings and young trees look very effective when planted in groups, especially where they are the same species. For example, a disused or rarely used siding on the layout will look good with a number of saplings growing alongside it.

Even at an early age trees can develop more than one trunk, and small saplings can look effective when modelled with twin trunks. The wire armatures in Fig. 185 are instantly turned into silver birch saplings with a coat of white paint; to complete the effect apply dark paint, stippled on to the trunks using a stiff-bristled paintbrush. Foliage can be added to suit the season.

Fig. 185: Saplings and young trees can look very effective when planted together in groups.

IVY-COVERED TREE TRUNKS

The remains of old tree trunks that are almost totally covered with ivy can sometimes be seen in country hedges or free-standing in fields, the majority of the original tree having long rotted away, except for a few remaining fine branches around the top of the trunk.

Trees like this can be made using wire, but as the trunk is not visible they are far easier to produce

Fig. 186: A large tree trunk almost completely covered with ivy.

Fig. 187: Naturally weathered wood is ideal for creating tree stumps.

Fig. 188: Cover the stump with glue where you want the ivy to be growing.

using a length of real wood. The wood can be either a man-made piece of dowel snapped to length to produce the look of a rotten trunk and painted to look like bark, or a real piece of dried-out branch can be used to great effect. If you want this type of tree to be free-standing, away from the hedge, it may be necessary to fix a planting pin to its base; this can be done by drilling a small hole in the base of the branch and inserting a small length of cocktail stick: the tree can then be fixed into a hole drilled into the baseboard.

In this demonstration a small piece of natural weathered wood has been allowed to dry out and has had a planting pin fixed into its base (*see* Fig. 187). Small holes have been drilled round the trunk towards its top (a pin or nail or something similar can be used if the wood is soft enough), and tiny off-cut pieces of Seamoss inserted into them and held in place with superglue. The Seamoss has had a light coat of mid-brown paint applied directly from an aerosol can.

If you choose to use a piece of smooth dowel, a layer of bark can be applied to the trunk, especially if any of it is to remain visible through the ivy.

Cover the stump with glue in the areas you want the ivy to be growing: load a paintbrush with neat PVA glue and apply it to the trunk, holding the trunk horizontal by its planting pin to avoid the glue dripping down the trunk and on to your fingers. Also paint some glue on to the joins where the Seamoss is fixed into the trunk, and a little way along the branch which is inserted into the hole (*see* Fig. 188). Leaving gaps in the glue will allow some of the natural trunk and dead wood to show through the ivy once the scatter representing it has been applied and the glue has dried.

Whilst the glue is still wet, apply a suitably coloured scatter or blend of scatters to the trunk, holding it over a sheet of paper to catch any that doesn't stick. Hold it by the pin and roll it round whilst applying the scatter with your other hand, so the scatter sticks to the glue all the way round the tree. Any loose scatter caught on the sheet of paper can be put back in the bag for later use. The whole trunk will benefit from an application of hairspray, as it will soak through the glue and scatter helping it to stick (*see* Fig. 189). Allow the glue to dry.

The tips of the Seamoss branches have been given a light covering of scatter, and the tree has been added to the hedge (*see* Fig. 190). It may be necessary to trim away some of the rubberized horsehair in the hedge to allow the trunk to be inserted. Use sharp scissors pushed into the hedge from above, and cut away any fibres that get in the way of the trunk; a little glue will help hold the trunk in place. The planting pin can be removed if the tree is used in the hedge, but if the tree is to be free-standing use the pin to hold the tree in place on the layout.

Fig. 189: Sprinkle liberal amounts of scatter on to the glue and spray the stump with hairspray.

Fig. 190: The natural effect of the stump can be appreciated once it has been added to the hedge.

Apply a little ivy scatter to the hedge in the immediate vicinity of the trunk to give the impression that it is growing rampantly through the hedge. To do this, apply glue to the hedge around the trunk using a paintbrush, and sprinkle on small amounts of ivy scatter.

Fig. 191 shows the effect of the completed hedge. The variations in the colours, density and height along the hedge all add to its realism. Once hedges like the one demonstrated here are blended into the rest of the groundwork and the surrounding scenery on the layout, the overall effect is even more striking.

SUMMARY

Not all mature hedges will contain all the elements shown in this chapter, but some may well do. Rubberized horsehair has been mixed with synthetic hair, Seamoss and wire to create a varied and realistic-looking hedge. A variety of scatter colours adds to the effect of a natural hedge. Hedges like the one demonstrated here can often be seen bordering country lanes, and it would be perfectly realistic to cut out gateways to fields in places along their length, with a rustic gatepost on each side of the gap.

Fig. 191: An overall view of the completed hedge.

Fig. 192: The narrow path is bordered by a thick hedge which consists mainly of mature hawthorns.

Fig. 193: The huge hedge round this field is no more than a row of carefully planted conifers. Note the fence posts made using railway sleepers, almost totally obscured by weeds.

Fig. 194: A small tree pokes through the top of this hedge.

Fig. 195: Not strictly a hedge, but this mass of ivy creates a great scenic feature and a useful screen.

John Farmer's P4 'Netherhope'. The great deal of foliage textures and colours add to the overgrown look of the hillside. The trees to the rear of the scene on either side of the lane actually touch, which is a common occurrence in nature. Broken fences, too, are common and add an interesting touch to the perimeter of the field. ANDY YORK AND BRM MAGAZINE

CHAPTER SEVEN

MATURE HEDGEROWS AND HEDGEROW TREES

Fig. 196: Part of a mature hedgerow complete with sign and telegraph pole.

Mature hedgerows are a common feature of the British countryside. Many follow boundaries originating hundreds of years ago, some dating back even to medieval times, and still dividing up farmland and bordering ancient lanes and pathways. They are more commonly seen in lowland Britain than in northern England and Scotland, where drystone walling is more prevalent. Mature hedgerows are often made up from a number of species, and include hedgerow trees.

The average height of the hedgerow modelled here is approximately 100mm (4in), though some stretches along its length are taller and some shorter; this equates to approximately 7m (25ft) in height in 'OO' gauge. Mature hedgerows designed for 'O'-gauge layouts could realistically be twice this height. As there can be a great variety of plant species evident in a mature hedgerow, similarly a variety of materials should be used along the length of the hedge to represent the different species of plant. It is also useful to have a good variety of scatters available to create different tones along the hedgerow.

Materials

- Wire or woody cuttings
- Masking tape
- Bark Powder
- Rubberized horsehair
- Canopy (synthetic hair)
- Paints
- Hairspray
- Scenic scatters
- Diluted PVA glue

Tools

- Wire cutters
- Paintbrushes
- Atomizer bottle
- Scissors

Fig. 197: A typical mature hedgerow borders each side of this country lane.

CREATING THE 'WOODY' FRAME FOR THE MATURE HEDGEROW

When creating mature hedgerows, rather than creating a framework solely from fine-fibred materials such as rubberized horsehair and synthetic hair, as with the hedge in the previous chapter, the main frame of the hedgerow looks best when created using stronger and thicker materials to give the impression that the hedge contains mature plants and small trees.

If you can source some woody offcuts from a privet hedge or similarly fine-branched plant, these are ideal for creating the framework for mature hedgerows, as are roots from garden shrubs (see Fig. 198). These should be washed and dried before use, and can be trimmed to size and shaped with secateurs or strong scissors to create the basic shape of the hedgerow; if possible cut them well in advance and let them dry out before use.

However, if sourcing such cuttings is not so easy, then use the following method.

Fig. 198: Natural pieces of root are useful for creating dead saplings amongst the greenery of the hedge as well as the armatures for the trees.

CREATING SMALL WIRE ARMATURES

This method involves creating small wire armatures to represent the trunks that often grow along the mature hedgerow. The art of creating tree armatures is covered in detail in the following chapters, and you would be advised to read through these before starting on your mature hedgerow.

Take a few lengths of fine wire; in this demonstration wire with 0.7mm and 1mm diameters are used, though you may choose to use finer or thicker wires, depending on the scale you are working in. For this hedge approximately twenty-five wires per armature are used, and the armatures will be 'planted' at roughly 50mm (2in) intervals. (Note that the number of wires used for each armature isn't critical, and the figure of twenty-five is just a guide.)

Start by tapping the bottoms of the wires on to a flat surface to create a flat end. Tightly wind some masking tape around the bottom of the wires to hold them together.

Next take a single wire and wind it around the wires in the trunk, working towards the top of the tree.

Next, pull five or so wires to one side to create small side branches. Twist the side branch and separate one or two wires from it to create finer side branches 'growing' from the first branch. Repeat this step until the five wires have been used to create a single side branch with five smaller branches growing from it (see Fig. 199).

Take another wire and create the same effect on the other side of the trunk, then repeat the process at the front and back of the trunk until all the wires have been used up. Obviously some side branches will be made using more or fewer than five wires each, and this will add variety to each armature once they are 'planted' together as a hedgerow (see Fig. 200). If you want you can create more side branches, each using fewer than five wires, but as these small trunks are really only to hold in place the other materials used for the hedge and are not particularly visible, they don't have to be of superb quality.

The trunks look more realistic if they are bent and shaped, rather than the wires being left perfectly straight; this can be done by hand or with the aid of pliers.

The trunks will benefit from a coat of bark; here, TREEMENDUS Bark Powder was applied to the armatures using a small paintbrush, and allowed to dry. Once dry, the bark was given a wash of dirty grey brown paint, and 'weathered' with weathering pigments (see Fig. 201).

Fig. 199: A simple side branch made using only five wires.

Fig. 200: The wire armatures for the hawthorns of the hedge.

Fig. 201: The hawthorn armatures are coated in bark and suitably weathered.

HEDGEROW TREES

Hedgerow trees, as their name suggests, are the large, mature trees that grow up through the tops of hedgerows. Many are left untrimmed so they grow to their full height, with a full spread of branches that provide shelter from the seasonal elements to the livestock in the fields. Traditionally they also provided a source of timber, firewood, and in some cases food.

Hedgerow trees are a common sight in the British landscape, and a valuable habitat for British wildlife. The most commonly planted species of hedgerow tree were oak and ash, and also elm, though many of these were either felled, or died due to Dutch elm disease in the late 1960s; however, for layouts based on an era before this time, the elm is the perfect choice of hedgerow tree.

It is possible to spot the remains of ancient hedgerows in the form of irregular lines of mature trees crossing open fields. These trees, when viewed from a certain point, are often seen to line up with each other, indicating they were once part of a hedgerow that has long been removed.

MAKING HEDGEROW TREES

In the same way that wire armatures are used for creating the 'woody' frame for the hedgerow, wire armatures are also a good choice for making hedgerow trees as they can be built to fit into a specific area where their shape and size may be governed by their surroundings. Alternatively, the trunks of hedgerow trees can be created using natural materials such as small pieces of privet, heather or sagebrush, which are trimmed accordingly to fit the scene.

This demonstration uses the more traditional wire armature method. The armature for the hedgerow tree is made in exactly the same way as the smaller armatures in the hedgerow, but it uses more wires, and its overall shape is more stylized, as ultimately it will be growing above the top of the hedge. Fig. 202 shows the finished tree armature, complete with bark and weathering: a detailed account of building trees such as the one used in this demonstration – and many other styles – is given in the following chapters (and not here, so as to avoid repetition).

THE BASE FOR THE HEDGEROW

The small wire armatures of the hedgerow and hedgerow trees are pushed into a thin strip of ceiling tile. The ceiling tile is the base for the bank of earth on which the hedgerow will be growing. Compressed paper ceiling tiles are very easy to cut and shape, and being soft and lightweight are the perfect material for this type of work. The strip of ceiling tile used as the base for this hedgerow has been painted using a mid-brown aerosol paint; matt brown emulsion paint is also ideal.

Next, diluted PVA is painted over the undercoat using a wide paintbrush, and a blend of TREEMENDUS Earth Powder, Forest Floor and scatter materials sprinkled on to the glue. This serves as a partially decorated scenic base on which the hedgerow may be built; once it has been positioned on the layout further details may be added and the hedgerow blended into its surroundings.

Incidentally ceiling tiles make a good base for all sorts of materials that can be found around railways: piles of ash, coal, ballast, rubble and soil can all be created by shaping small pieces of tile, which can then be covered in a very thin layer of any scenic material.

Fig. 202: Hedgerow tree wire armature.

Fig. 203: Hawthorns fixed into a raised bank.

Position the wire armatures along the top of the ceiling tile at slightly irregular intervals but in a fairly straight line (*see* Fig. 203); they can be held in place with glue to keep them secure – a little spot of PVA, superglue or grab adhesive will work well. Note that two of the wire armatures here have had ivy added, growing up their trunks.

HEDGEROW DETAILS

CREATING BRAMBLES

Naturally, over time, some of the small trees and bushes growing in hedgerows die back, and this occasionally leaves gaps between the trunks of the bushes, shrubs and trees that make up the hedgerow; in turn these gaps are often quickly colonized by brambles and other plants. When making long lengths of hedgerow, leaving irregular gaps between some of the trunks allows you to introduce areas of brambles and suchlike growing amongst the trunks.

To create brambles, take a little canopy (synthetic hair) and tease it apart using your fingers to make small mounds; first spray the mounds with a dark-coloured paint from an aerosol as this will make the fibres more rigid and therefore stronger, then spray them with hairspray and apply a fine scatter – a blend of complementary dark and light scatters has

been used on the brambles in this demonstration. The brambles have been placed in position along the bottom of the hedgerow with a spot of PVA to hold them in place, then sprayed with scenic glue or diluted PVA to secure the scatter.

MAKING FENCE POSTS

Fence posts can also be put in amongst the brambles with just their tops sticking out, giving the impression the hedgerow has been made more secure using fencing. The fence posts used along this hedgerow are simply cocktail sticks cut to approximately 30mm (1in) in length. The sticks have been painted and inserted into small holes pre-made in the ceiling tile using a sharpened wooden skewer, leaving approximately 20mm (¾in) visible above ground level; a spot of glue holds the posts in place (*see* Fig. 204).

MAKING THE HEDGEROW FOLIAGE

Whilst the glue holding the armatures in place is drying, create the foliage by taking some rubberized horsehair and teasing it apart, making a very open and airy structure (*see* Fig. 205). The more you pull apart the rubberized horsehair, the more open the foliage structures will be; this means that the armatures holding them up will be more visible. This hedgerow uses an approximately 19sq cm (3sq in) block.

Fig. 204: The initial layer of groundwork and fence posts added to the bank.

Spray the rubberized horsehair very lightly with black or dark brown paint directly from an aerosol tin; give it a second coat using a mid-brown paint to highlight its outer branches. The darkness of the first coat of black paint will represent shade within the hedge once it is complete, and will add much depth to it visually. This method of shading can also be applied to tree canopies, dense brambles and other foliage created using rubberized horsehair and other fibrous materials. Note the difference in both colour and texture between the painted piece and the original block (see Fig. 206).

Give the painted, rubberized horsehair a liberal spray of hairspray, and sprinkle it with a scenic scatter. The rubberized horsehair can have scenic glue or diluted PVA sprayed directly over it using a bottle with an atomizer, without the need to use hairspray initially, but it is more difficult to gauge the amount of scatter being added to the glue. Take a green scatter and apply it liberally to the hairspray; here, 'Midsummer' scatter is used. A spray of scenic glue and further hairspray over the scatter will help the glue soak in. Repeat the application of hairspray, scatter and glue to all the rubberized horsehair components for the hedge. Apply a little scattering of a complementary colour to add highlights to the foliage: see Fig. 207 – the glue is still wet in this photograph.

The hedge being modelled here is based on a mature hawthorn hedge as it appears in May, which allows for some white flowers to be added to the green foliage. Apply a light spray of scenic glue and carefully apply the white scatter to the foliage canopy. Sometimes hawthorn can be completely covered with flowers, and the amount of white scatter you add is a personal choice (see Fig. 208). Certain varieties of hawthorn have deep pink/crimson-coloured flowers, which also look effective when portrayed in model form.

Allow the hedge canopy to dry before placing it carefully on to the wire armatures, teasing the fibres further apart if necessary. Some of the white/pink scatter will inevitably fall on to the brambles growing in the gaps below the trees, but carefully pick this off, to help differentiate the brambles from the hedge canopy.

Fig. 205: Tease apart the rubberized horsehair.

Fig. 206: The rubberized horsehair is painted with aerosol paint.

Fig. 207: Painted horsehair covered with scatter.

Fig. 208: Canopies of foliage are added to the hawthorns.

When the hedge foliage is in place, trim any over-long fibres and generally tidy up the canopy. When you are happy with the look of the hedgerow so far, spray the whole thing with diluted PVA glue to ensure the canopy sticks to the armatures.

MAKING THE CANOPIES FOR THE HEDGEROW TREES

The hedgerow tree will be less densely covered in foliage than the hedge, but its canopy is created using the same principles and techniques as for the foliage on the hedge: teased apart, rubberized horse-hair or synthetic hair, covered with scatter (*see* Fig.

209). Use a scatter or blend of scatters for the tree foliage that is different in colour from that used for the hedge: this will add variety to the hedgerow, and additional contrast to the overall landscape.

Make more canopy for both the hedge and the hedgerow tree than you actually require. The remainder will be used later once the hedge is almost finished, to fill some of the spaces between the individual trunks.

The canopy can be attached in two ways: either apply a little neat PVA glue to the branch tips and carefully add the tree canopy, making sure the fibres come into contact with the glue. Alternatively add the foliage and then spray the tree with diluted PVA glue: this will not only stick the canopy to the armature, but will help strengthen the canopy even further. Allow the hedge and tree canopies to dry.

Once the tree has dried it can be tidied up in the same way the hedge was, by removing long fibres and any hoops of fibre visible in the canopy. When you are happy with the look of the tree it can be inserted into the hedgerow; a little superglue or PVA will hold it in place.

In certain instances it is best to glue the wire tree armature in position in the hedgerow and then add the canopy; once it is among the other plants in the hedge this avoids causing any damage to the tree or the hedgerow, especially if the spot where the tree is growing is a tight fit (*see* Fig. 210).

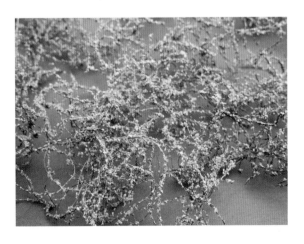

Fig. 209: Teased apart canopy for the hedgerow tree.

Fig. 210: The hedgerow tree is fixed into the bank.

Fig. 211: A dead sapling sticking through the top of a hedgerow.

ADDING THE DETAILS

In mature hedgerows there are often small saplings growing through the hedge foliage, and sometimes the remains of dead saplings and small trees can also be seen. Small wire armatures can be fashioned to represent dead trees and saplings, as can natural pieces of weathered wood or fibrous roots.

CREATING DEAD SAPLINGS USING NATURAL ROOT

To create dead saplings using natural root, wash off any soil that may be present on the selected piece of root and allow it to dry. It can then be given a light undercoat of paint, applied using an aerosol, airbrush or paintbrush. Cut the 'trunk' of the root to a length that will allow the fine branches at the top of the sapling to protrude from the hedgerow once it has been planted among the hawthorns. Remove any other bits of unwanted root using a sharp blade (see Fig. 212); put the offcuts to one side as they can be used elsewhere in the hedgerow.

Dead trees and saplings lose most of their fine branches after they die, so the majority of the fine roots should be removed from the main trunk. Use sharp scissors or a sharp blade to do this, but snap the thicker ones by hand if possible so it looks as if they have broken off naturally (see Fig. 213).

The bark at the very tips of the branches can be stripped off: use your thumbnail to remove it. If necessary use a little light-coloured paint to highlight the dead heartwood at the ends of the snapped branches; do this before weathering the root so the light-coloured paint doesn't look too artificial. The root can be weathered using paints or weathering pigments to give it a natural-looking finish; be sure to blend the bark and the heartwood together (see Fig. 214).

Fig. 212: Remove the unwanted 'branches' from the real piece of root.

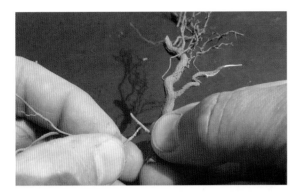

Fig. 213: Snapping some of the branches results in a realistic weathered effect.

Fig. 214: The sapling should be weathered to complement the other trees in the hedgerow.

Once the roots have completely dried they can be added to the hedgerow. Make a small hole in the base between the trunks of the hawthorn using a wooden skewer, and carefully insert the end of the dead sapling; a spot of superglue will hold it secure (see Fig. 215). Some of the offcuts have been weathered in the same way as the main sapling and also fixed into the hedgerow.

TIDYING THE TREE AND HEDGE FOLIAGE

Any final tidying of the tree and hedge foliage can be done at this stage. Use sharp scissors to remove any long flyaway fibres still remaining on the hedge, and any fibres that create a hoop (see Fig. 216). Put the cuttings to one side as they will almost certainly be useful for the details of the groundwork beneath the hedge in the next step.

Small pieces of natural wood are useful for filling the gaps in between the trunks; this piece has been given a coat of bark, which has then been weathered. It has been planted amongst the hedgerow trunks to represent a long-dead tree stump (see Fig. 217): a wire planting pin was pushed into the bottom of the trunk, which was then simply pushed into the soft ceiling tile. The stump could also be dressed with ivy-coloured scatter to match the two hawthorns in the hedgerow.

Fig. 215: Fix the sapling into the hedgerow, holding it in place with a little glue.

Fig. 216: Remove any unnatural strands of foliage using sharp scissors.

Fig. 217: A weathered stump is also added to the bank.

BLENDING IN THE BANK

Assuming the hedgerow is going to be added to the layout bordering a field, the bank on which the hedge is growing will probably need to be blended into its surroundings. The blending-in process will be much easier and will look more realistic if the materials used in the immediate area around the hedge are used to blend the bank into the rest of the groundwork (see Fig. 218).

Take some of the Raw Grass fibres that will be used for the field and add them to the mound. Use a paintbrush to apply PVA glue in patches to the bank where you want the grass to be growing. Chop some of the fibres into tiny pieces and work them into the glue with a wooden skewer (see Fig. 219) – however, don't cover the bank completely, but leave some of the existing groundwork visible through it. Using more than one colour of fibre gives a better result to the groundwork. Apply fewer grass fibres to the bank the further in you go towards the trunks. Finally sprinkle a little Earth Powder over the grass and into the glue.

Fig. 218: Some of the materials used to help the groundwork below the hedgerow blend in with its surroundings.

Fig. 219: Work the chopped fibres into the glue using a wooden skewer.

BRINGING IT ALL TOGETHER

Sometimes it is the very subtle features of the landscape, which are not always immediately noticeable, that add an element of realism to the landscape. Rabbit burrows in the bank are easy to create, here by simply pushing a pointed skewer into the soft ceiling tile (see Fig. 220); a pencil can be used to make bigger holes if you wish to represent a fox's den or a badger's sett, for example.

Two tiny rooks' nests have been created and glued to the top of the dead sapling (see Fig. 221). To make nests, take a small pinch of synthetic hair and roll it into a tiny ball; add a spot of glue to the branch, and carefully sit the nest on to the glue. If you leave the ball whole, like the nests here, they can be used to represent crows' nests or squirrels' dreys.

Signposts and telegraph poles also make interesting features when they are seen poking through the tops of hedgerows (see Fig. 222). The telegraph pole used in this demonstration has been glued into a little hole in the ceiling tile. The base of the pole has been blended into the surrounding groundwork using finely chopped Raw Grass fibres. Telegraph poles in the real world are invariably never 100 per cent vertical, so there is no reason to worry too much about getting them totally upright on our models, either.

The spare canopy made earlier when the foliage was being assembled for the hedge and tree has also been introduced to the base of the trunks. It has been worked in among the trunks, again using a wooden skewer from behind, and held in place with PVA (see Fig. 223); the fence posts are still just visible through the horsehair. When the horsehair is in the correct position, lightly spray it with diluted PVA and apply a very light sprinkling of fine scatter in small patches to add to the variety of tones already in the hedgerow. Small pieces of root have also been glued into the undergrowth, some vertically and some horizontally, to give the appearance of branches that have fallen from the trees above.

The final step in creating mature hedgerows is to fill some of the spaces between the trunks with scenic materials, which in turn will bring all the elements of the hedgerow together. Finely chopped

Fig. 220: Rabbit burrows add a touch of character to the bank.

Fig. 221: A couple of rooks' nests add to the natural look of the hedgerow.

Fig. 222: The telegraph pole adds interest to the hedgerow and shows the scale of the trees in it.

Fig. 223: Further groundwork is carefully added and held in place with a spot of glue.

Fig. 224: Raw Grass fibres help to blend the brambles into their surroundings.

Raw Grass fibres are added to the groundwork to help blend the brambles into the base (see Fig. 224). Apply a little diluted PVA in the areas you require the fibres and work them in with a wooden skewer, making sure they come into contact with the glue.

To add a fleck of colour, a small group of poppies has been added to the base (see Fig. 225). Take a tiny amount of glue on a paintbrush and dab it on to the very tips of one of the groups of long Raw Grass fibres, then carefully add a small pinch of coloured scatter, removing any that doesn't adhere

to the glue. A few pale-coloured bristles, trimmed off an old paintbrush, have also been glued into the brambles.

In the final photograph, all the individual elements of the hedgerow appear to be growing naturally (see Fig. 226). Note that when mature hedgerows such as the one modelled here are seen in a natural landscape, they sometimes have large spaces in them, and are often nothing more than small islands of hedgerow that follow a common line across the landscape.

Fig. 225: Flowers add a tiny splash of colour to the groundwork.

Fig. 226: The finished hedgerow. With care, a lot of detail can be added even into the smallest of areas.

Fig. 227: Note the various shapes, textures and colours in this mature hedgerow.

Fig. 228: A natural mature hedgerow; you can just see the fence hidden among the trunks and weeds.

Fig. 229: The foliage and trees around this tunnel mouth dwarf it completely.

Fig. 230: A mature row of trees creates a superb backdrop for the trains in this view. Note, too, the huge variety of colour in the foliage on the embankment in the foreground.

John de Frayssinet's 009-gauge 'Cliffhanger'. The height of this unusual layout from the coastline at the bottom of the baseboard to the top of the mountain creates a dramatic scene. A vast area of the landscape is covered with a single, dense canopy of tree foliage, whilst the remaining scenics are modelled beautifully as weed-covered sandstone. The wooden bridge adds a man-made feature to the landscape. This layout is another great example of a railway running through a natural-looking landscape. ANDY YORK AND BRM MAGAZINE

CHAPTER EIGHT

OAK AND BROADLEAF TREES

Materials

- Wire
- Aluminium tube (for the planting pin, which is optional)
- Superglue
- Masking tape
- Bark Powder
- Rubberized horsehair
- Paints
- Hairspray
- Scenic scatters
- Diluted PVA glue

Tools

- Wire cutters
- Paintbrushes
- Atomizer bottle
- Scissors

Trees are amongst the largest and longest-living organisms on the planet. Some species grow very closely packed together, forming dense forests with impossibly straight trunks, whilst others grow in solitude in open fields with a huge rounded crown with very even growth. Trees can sometimes be sculpted by the action of the wind, which causes the formation of sometimes incredibly beautiful, twisted windswept trunks and a minimal amount of living foliage on the tree's branches.

Trees grow in most areas of the UK, and if at all possible at least one should be included on your layout, if only to highlight the scale of the composition.

TREE CHARACTERISTICS

All trees start life as tiny seeds, cuttings or grafts, but the size they ultimately grow to is something which is often overlooked, especially when it comes to making scale models of them. As an example, a tree of 30m (100ft) in height, which is big but not uncommon, in 'OO' (4mm to the foot) would be 400mm (almost 16in) in height; therefore a 15m (50ft) tree – which is not very big at all for a mature tree – would be 200mm (almost 8in) in height. An interesting example, which all 'OO' railway modellers can instantly identify with, is that a tree standing 19m (63ft 6in) in height is as tall as a 'OO' British Railways Mark 1 carriage stood on its end. It is fair to point out that not all trees are as tall as 18-plus metres (60-plus feet), but many of the trees we see in the landscape are. The trees pictured towering above the building in Fig. 231 ably demonstrate this point.

Trees of different species have differing growth patterns. The individual shape of trees can also be determined by the environment they grow in, and being able to capture these attributes will produce model trees that really do look like the species typical of the environment they are to be 'planted' in.

English oaks often have very thick trunks and heavy boughs, with many irregular bends. They often lose some of their boughs during times of drought as they mature in order to keep themselves alive, which is the reason why mature oak trees often have a distinctive rounded shape with the occasional dead branch sticking out from the foliage. As they mature their bark becomes rough and fissured.

Although all the above is true it will probably be all but impossible to find two trees of the same species that are identical, but they will always have certain common features which make them recognizable as the trees they are.

Fig. 231: Large mature trees to the rear of Summerseat station on the East Lancs Railway completely dominate the landscape.

THE CONSTRUCTION OF MODEL TREES

There are many ways in which to approach the construction of model trees. Wire armatures produce the best results as they can be styled to fit in a certain space, to a precise size, and with branches starting at any point on the trunk from ground level to almost its top. These simple facts mean that by using wire to create trees, we can style them into any species of tree we want and to almost any size, too.

This chapter takes a detailed look at creating a tree, in this example an oak, using 100 separate strands of wire which are twisted together and styled into the shape of an oak tree. This wire armature is then coated with a realistic bark mixture. Once the bark has dried the trunk is painted and 'weathered', and finally foliated using various techniques to give it the typical appearance of its species.

CONSTRUCTING THE WIRE ARMATURE

In this demonstration, the tree created is to be styled at approximately 254mm (10in) in height – which at 4mm to the foot means that it represents a tree 19m (63ft) in height, the approximate length of a Mark 1 carriage.

This demonstration uses 100 wires (*see* Fig. 232), each of them 30cm (12in) in length and 0.7mm in diameter. The steps in this demonstration assume we are making only one tree from the wires, but they can be snipped in half prior to commencing work on the tree, producing 200 15cm (6in) wires, allowing you to style two or more smaller trees using the same original 100 wires and the identical technique.

Fig. 232: A hundred wires are used in the construction of this oak tree.

Fig. 233: Tap the wires on a hard surface to create a flat end.

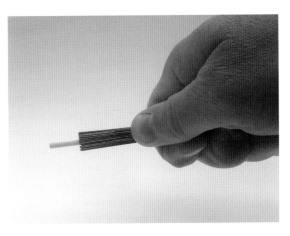

Fig. 234: Create a planting pin by pulling a few wires out from the 'trunk'.

Remove the masking tape from both ends of the wires. Loosely take hold of the wires in your fist and gently tap one end on to a flat surface. This will result in a flat end to the grip of wires (see Fig. 233).

To form a planting pin, carefully pull out a few strands of wire from the centre and wrap them in two layers of masking tape (see Fig. 234). Wrap the tape around the wires tightly, as this will form the anchor for the tree, which will hold it securely on your layout.

MAKING A ROOT STRUCTURE

An optional feature to add to your tree is a root structure. Not all trees have a large spread of roots showing on the surface of the ground, but when a model tree is built with one, it does add to its appearance.

Wrap a couple of layers of masking tape around the trunk (see Fig. 235) approximately 15mm (½in) up from the ends of the wires at the planting pin end of the tree.

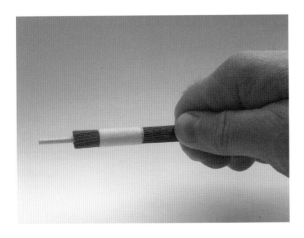

Fig. 235: Initially a small amount of masking tape helps hold the trunk together.

Fig. 236: Optionally, roots can be created at the foot of the tree.

Next, using your fingers or a pair of pliers, bend the wires between the planting pin and the bottom of the tape on the trunk upwards and outwards to give the trunk a characteristic root flare. The wires can be left simply flared at the base of the tree, or can be twisted together as in Fig. 236 to create individual roots spreading outwards from the tree's lower trunk, to give the impression they are holding the tree firmly in the ground. Note how the wires that are not used to create the roots have been pushed up and into the trunk so their ends are flush with the bottom of the tree. The planting pin has also been pushed a little further into the centre of the trunk.

Take one of the wires (Wire A) and pull it away from the main bunch ensuring it does not pull away from the root system. Starting low down the trunk, wind Wire A so that it spirals up what will become the lower trunk. Be sure to pull this wire tight as it is this wire that helps hold the trunk together.

MAKING THE BRANCHES

At this stage it is useful if you know roughly where you want the first (the lowest) branch on the tree to be positioned (see Fig. 237). If the tree is being designed to hide something on the layout, a fiddle yard exit for instance, then it is advisable to start the branches fairly low down the trunk; if, on the other hand, the tree is designed to draw the eye towards another interesting view along the layout, it may be necessary to start the branches slightly higher up the trunk to allow the viewer a clear line of sight to what lies in the distance.

When you reach the point on the trunk where you want the first bough to be growing from, take approximately fifteen wires and bend them away from the main trunk; these wires will form the first bough and side branches of your tree (see Fig. 238). Continue winding Wire A, but now wind it round the fifteen wires that are protruding from the trunk for about 20mm (1in) or so, and not the trunk itself.

Pull four or five wires (Wires B, C, D, E) to one side of the 'bough', and continue winding the original wire (Wire A) around these four: these wires will become the first side branch (that is, Wires A, B, C, D and E). Split the wires making up the side branch into twos or threes, winding them around each other as you work along the branch (for instance A and B together, and C, D and E together), as shown in the line drawing (see Fig. 239).

When all the wires have been used and they are separated into single wires, take another wire (Wire F) and repeat the process using four wires a little further along the bough but this time on the opposite side of the bough to the first side branch. Work along the bough using fewer wires per side branch as

Fig. 237: Decide where you want the first branch to be 'growing' from.

Fig. 238: Pull a few wires to one side: these create the lowest bough.

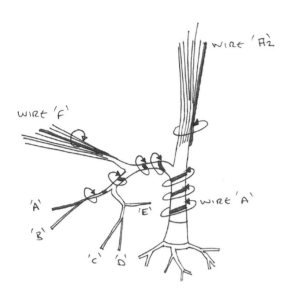

Fig. 239: Line drawing showing branch formation.

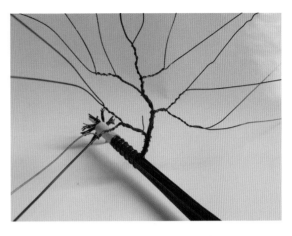

Fig. 240: The first branch is complete: the wires just need trimming to length.

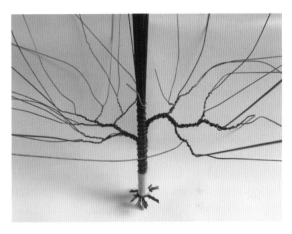

Fig. 241: A branch is formed on the opposite side of the trunk to the first branch.

Fig. 242: More branches are created around the trunk, creating a balanced-looking tree.

you work along it, until all the wires have been used up (*see* Fig. 240).

Next take a new wire from the trunk (Wire A2) and wrap it in a spiralling motion around the trunk, pulling it tightly in exactly the same way as Wire A. Pulling the wires tight around the trunk also creates a good taper to the tree's trunk. In this demonstration another bough has been created a little higher up the tree but on the opposite side of the trunk (*see* Fig. 241): this creates an evenly balanced tree on which to add the foliage.

The next steps involve repeating the process set out above. The third bough in this demonstration is positioned towards the rear of the trunk, but only uses twelve wires. The fourth bough also uses twelve wires, and is positioned at the front of the trunk (*see* Fig. 242). The spacing between the boughs should decrease slightly the further up the tree you get

Branches and boughs get thinner as they get higher up the tree's trunk, and this is the reason for using fewer wires as you proceed further up the trunk. The number of wires per bough is a guide only: it is not critical and there is no need to count

Fig. 243: All 100 wires have now been incorporated into the tree's trunk and branch system.

out individual wires. Typically boughs five and six would require ten wires each, boughs seven and eight, eight wires, boughs nine and ten could use five and three wires respectively, and the apex of the tree could end with the final two wires.

The armature is complete once all the wires have been used and formed into branches. There is still a lot of work to do, but the basic outline of the tree can be seen amongst the long wires (see Fig. 243). Note the realistic taper to the trunk.

SHAPING THE ARMATURE

The armature must now be shaped. Take a pair of wire cutters and whilst still considering the overall shape of the tree, start snipping the long wires down to a length that will suit the size and scale of the tree you are creating. If the tree is to be given a canopy of foliage, as in this demonstration, some of the wires can be left overly long, according to your design – so if your tree appears to be getting too narrow towards the top and you envisage a well-rounded, dome-shaped tree, the wires can be left fairly long as they will be mostly hidden by foliage. The wires shown in Fig. 244 have been trimmed to a length of approximately 10–15mm (¼–½in).

All the wires have now been trimmed to length, and the resulting structure is well suited to the shape of the oak tree being demonstrated. Note, too, that the trunk has been subtly bent by hand to give it a more appealing and natural-looking shape than the previous photograph (see Fig. 245). Note how the main boughs on this armature are on the outside of the bends in the trunk, something which occurs in nature. Small details such as this will add to the realism of your trees.

Now the surplus wires have been trimmed away from the armature the boughs themselves will also

Fig. 244: The long wires are trimmed to make a more tree-like shape.

Fig. 245: The trunk is shaped to add more character to the tree.

Fig. 246: The side branches are also bent and fashioned to represent an old oak tree.

Fig 247: An aluminium planting pin is glued on to the base of the tree trunk.

benefit from the addition of bends and kinks (see Fig. 246). These bends needn't be too extreme: even subtle changes to their shape will add to the look of the tree. The boughs and side branches have been positioned to loosely emulate the branches on the tree in Fig. 14 (in Chapter 1).

Offcuts of wire are very useful for making the kind of fallen boughs that are associated with old English oak trees. Put all your offcuts to one side for use later.

REINFORCING THE PLANTING PIN

The next task is to superglue a small length of copper or aluminium tube to the planting pin formed at the base of the trunk (see Fig. 247). This pin will hold the tree in place on the layout. Pins like this are useful if your trees are likely to require moving away from the layout at any time, for maintenance or when they are part of an exhibition layout, for example. A short length of tube with an internal diameter that equals the external diameter of the pin attached to the tree can be fixed into the baseboard, so the tree's pin fits snugly inside it.

IMPROVING THE LOOK OF THE LOWER TRUNK

There are two ways in which the wire spiralling the trunk (Wire A) can be treated: both methods will improve the look of the lower trunk. The first method involves actually removing Wire A from the trunk, and is the one to choose if you want to keep the trunk narrow and smooth. Take your wire cutters and carefully snip Wire A at its lowest point on the trunk, close to the roots, and also where it joins the first bough. Then unwind the loose piece of wire and discard it.

The second method, the one used here, involves covering the trunk and lower boughs with short lengths – 50 to 75mm (2 to 3in) – of masking tape (see Fig. 248); these are wrapped tightly round the trunk and lower boughs. Not only is this a useful practice for hiding the wires, it is also a very good method of adding more girth to the trunk, which is especially relevant when making a large oak tree, for example. In Fig. 249 masking tape completely covers the trunk and main boughs.

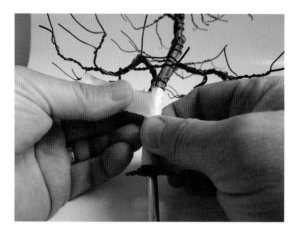

Fig. 248: The lower trunk has masking tape applied to it, to give extra girth to the tree.

Fig. 249: The tree's trunk and main boughs have been totally covered with masking tape.

ADDING A LAYER OF BARK

When the masking tape has been added and the required thickness of trunk achieved, a layer of bark is applied to the armature, which will transform the bare wires into something actually resembling the bark of a tree. The bark coating used in this demonstration is TREEMENDUS Bark Powder mixed with a little diluted PVA glue to the ratio of three parts water to one part PVA – though not too much of the diluted glue is needed, and it is advisable to add

Fig. 250: The bark's consistency should be such that it just sticks to the mixing stick.

it to the powder a few drops at a time. If the mix is too runny the bark mixture will not cover the wires on the tree enough and they will show through when the bark has dried. If the mix is too thick it will be very difficult to apply to the armature with a brush. The perfect consistency is one that sticks to the mixing stick without being too runny or too thick and heavy (see Fig. 250).

Starting at the top of the tree (so you can hold the trunk whilst you add the bark), apply the bark mixture using a paintbrush (see Fig. 251). For some of the finer branches, the ones that use only two or three wires, it is advisable to dilute a little of the bark mixture only *slightly* more than the recommended consistency. As the more diluted mixture is painted onto the finer branches it will flow from the brush and cover the wires very easily.

The thicker, less diluted bark mixture is used for all the other larger branches, boughs, trunk and root system. The mixture can be applied to the trunk fairly thickly and stippled with the tip of the brush as work proceeds around it. The detail of the bark on the trunk can be enhanced even further by dragging a toothbrush or stiff-bristled paintbrush vertically down it when the bark has almost dried: this will create the effect of rough-textured bark, which will look especially good after the bark has been painted and weathered. In Fig. 252 the armature has

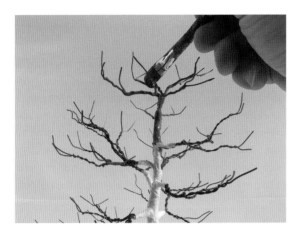

Fig. 251: Starting at the top of the tree, add the bark to the armature. Dilute the bark fractionally more if necessary for the finer branches.

Fig. 252: The tree armature after it has been covered with bark and allowed to dry.

been completely coated with the bark mixture and allowed to dry. Drying takes approximately twenty-four hours, allowing the bark coating to set into a very realistic-looking and durable finish.

If any blobs of bark are evident on the branch tips they can easily be removed by pinching them off with a thumb and forefinger. It is often unnecessary to cover all the single wires at the end of the branches with bark, especially when the tree is going to be covered

in a mass of foliage. Instead it is best to spray them with aerosol paint, or paint applied using an airbrush: colours ranging from mid to dark brown and black are fine. The paint also takes the metallic look away from the snipped ends of the wire without thickening them up at all (see Fig. 253), and will blend them into the rest of the tree. Avoid getting too much paint on the bark-coated branches and trunk, as they have paint applied with a brush in the next step.

Fig. 253: Remove any blobs of bark present on the branch tips and spray lightly with an appropriately coloured paint.

Fig. 254: What colour isn't bark? A huge variety of colour and texture is evident on this real tree trunk.

PAINTING THE TRUNK AND BRANCHES

The next step is to give the trunk and branch system a wash of colour to represent the various different colours that can be present on tree trunks. Tree trunks can be all manner of colours depending on where they are growing, whether they are wet or dry, and what is growing on the bark of the particular tree in question.

The tree in this demonstration has been given a light wash with a blend of Sap Green, Yellow Ochre, black, Raw Umber and grey acrylic paints, which have been diluted with clean water in a ratio of approximately ten parts water to one part paint. There is no definitive paint wash to colour tree trunks with, but bear in mind they are rarely brown and are more often a grey/green colour. Dab the paint on to the branches and trunk. To add randomness to the look of the tree, apply the paint to some of the branches first, then the trunk, then back to the branches.

Whilst the paint is still wet, take some neat or slightly diluted green paint and dab it on to the areas where you want more prominent algae effects. The same can be done with black/dark grey paint, too; just a tiny amount here and there will add to the overall effect (see Fig. 255).

Moss can grow on any side and indeed every side of the same tree, depending on its environment, and mossy effects can easily be added to the tree at this stage. Take some neat PVA glue on a brush and carefully apply it to the parts of the tree where you want the moss to be growing; around the root system and in the crooks of the lower boughs are likely places to find moss growing. Next, sprinkle very fine scatter over the glue, flattening it down with your finger if necessary (see Fig. 256). If the scatter needs toning down a little, use some of the diluted paint that was used for weathering the main trunk and branches. Put the armature to one side and allow the glue to dry.

CREATING THE CANOPY

There are various materials and a variety of methods we can adopt to make our tree canopies, and what we do depends upon the species and style of tree being created. For broadleaved tree canopies being modelled in leaf, rubberized horsehair is an ideal material as it is easily teased apart to create open structures, and is a durable, long-lasting material (see Fig. 257).

Take a block of rubberized horsehair and pull at it so as to tear it apart. The more the fibres of the block

Fig. 255: The trunk and branches have been weathered using a variety of acrylic paints.

Fig. 256: Scatter can be added to the trunk to represent thick moss growing on the bark.

are pulled apart, the more open the final canopy will appear. Once the desired density of canopy has been achieved it is improved by a light coat of paint from an aerosol can or airbrush. This paint is simply to tone down the colour of the rubberized fibres and should ideally match the finer branches on the wire armature (see Fig. 258).

Tease apart and lightly paint enough rubberized horsehair to cover the whole tree. It can be a good practice to style small pieces to fit a particular bough of the armature, working on small parts of the tree at a time, but with care the whole tree canopy can be created in one go. For this tree, two long sections of canopy which will 'wrap' around the branches have been made, one for the upper section of the tree and one for the lower section (see Fig. 259).

At this point it is worth noting that tree canopies vary enormously, with some appearing incredibly dense (see Fig. 260) and others very open, with clear daylight visible through their structure (see Fig. 261).

Take the pieces of rubberized horsehair and carefully place them on the wire armature, working them into the framework of branches (see Fig. 262); avoid packing it too tightly if you want an open-structured tree. There is no need to be overly concerned about how neat it looks at this stage, nor to add any glue to hold the canopy in place yet, either.

The next stage is to add the scatter, and it is best to have the following items to hand before you begin: hairspray, scatters, a sheet of newspaper, and a bottle of diluted PVA with an atomizer attached. Apply a liberal spray of hairspray to the rubberized horsehair, making sure it reaches inside the structure; spray the tree from above and below as well as from the sides. This is easily done by holding the planting pin in one hand and turning the tree, and using the other hand to spray it with the hairspray.

Whilst the hairspray is still wet, take the scatter and carefully sprinkle it over the tree; then turn the structure over and apply more scatter to the underside. Do this over the sheet of newspaper so you can reuse any scatter that doesn't stick to the tree. Mix in a slightly darker-coloured scatter to give the impression of shade to the undersides of the canopy foliage, and a small amount of a lighter-

Fig. 257: Rubberized horsehair in its 'out of the box' appearance.

Fig. 258: Spray the horsehair to tone it down a little, ideally with the same paint as used for the fine branches of the tree.

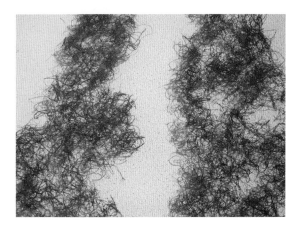

Fig. 259: Two long, airy pieces of horsehair are used to create the very fine foliage branches for this tree.

Fig. 260: A natural tree with a very densely growing canopy of foliage.

coloured scatter for the upper areas of the tree to give the impression of new fresh leaves growing in the canopy. Any scatter that sticks to the branches or trunk can be simply brushed off using a paintbrush with stiff bristles.

The whole tree can now be given a spray with scenic glue or PVA glue diluted in a ratio of three parts water to one of glue. Give the whole tree a good soaking with the glue using a bottle with an atomizer – an old kitchen cleaner bottle or something similar is ideal; be sure to spray clean water through it after use to stop it clogging up. Apply another liberal spray of hairspray as this will help the glue to soak into the scatter. The spray of glue also helps the canopy stick to the armature. More scatter can be added at this stage, whilst the glue is still wet, to areas that look a little short of foliage (see Fig. 263).

Fig. 261: A foliage canopy of a very open and airy structure.

Fig. 262: Rubberized horsehair added to the tree armature. The density of this tree will be somewhere in between that shown in the two previous photographs.

Fig. 263: Scatter is applied to the rubberized horsehair then liberally sprayed with glue, which helps hold it in place.

Fig. 264: The glue will dry to create a very durable tree canopy with a matt finish.

Avoid getting too much glue on to the trunk or lower branches, and where possible dab any from the trunk with a damp, lint-free cloth. The tree is best set aside for twenty-four hours or so until the glue has dried.

After twenty-four hours or so at normal room temperature the tree's foliage canopy should have completely dried, and any whiteness from the glue should have disappeared and dried to a strong matt finish (see Fig. 264).

REFINING THE TREE

Once all is dry, the canopy can be refined to make it into a specimen tree. Take a pair of sharp scissors and trim any over-long strands of rubberized horsehair that protrude from the tree (see Fig. 265), particularly on the undersides of the boughs. In nature the fine branches of mature oak and other broadleaved trees don't generally hang below the main boughs, which are often fairly flat underneath; this is due in part to the fact that new growth generally grows upwards towards the light, giving these trees the appearance of rounded mounds of foliage sitting on the main branches.

Any 'loops' of fibre visible in the canopy should also be cut (see Fig. 266). Rather than simply cutting a

loop with your scissors, it is best to actually remove a small section of the loop. This will create two separate branches and disguise the fact that the two branches were ever joined at all (see Fig. 267).

It is worth taking your time over this step, as this is the final refinement stage. It is likely that some scatter will fall from the tree whilst it is being handled and trimmed; this is to be expected, as not all the scatter will have come into direct contact with the glue. When all the loops have been dealt with and

Fig. 265: Remove any over-long fibres using sharp scissors.

Fig. 266: Sometimes there are fibres in the canopy that bend around forming loops.

Fig. 267: Create two branches by removing a small section of the loops.

all the long flyaway and dangling fibres have been removed, finish the tree by applying a further spray with diluted PVA and hairspray; more scatter can also be added where necessary. The resulting tree will be very strong and long-lasting.

Young trees growing in the wild often have foliage canopies that start at ground level, with very little or even no trunk or branch structure visible at all (see Fig. 268); they can also be very irregular in their shape. Even the trunks of mature trees growing in the wild can be totally hidden by foliage. Trees, shrubs and bushes like this can be made using

a very simple wire armature covered with rubberized horsehair.

Some trees, however, have trunks that are visible from ground level all the way up to their apex, like the mature sycamore in Fig. 269. Note that this particular tree is as wide as it is tall.

Fig. 270 shows the completed oak tree, which has been styled on the tree growing in the field opposite Irwell Vale Halt. The foliage canopy could be opened up even more by carefully trimming into the rubberized horsehair using sharp scissors to reveal the branch system and trunk.

Fig. 268: The foliage of copper beech makes a striking contrast to the general greens of the scenery. The trunk on this tree is totally obscured.

Fig. 269: This mature sycamore has most of its trunk visible from this angle.

Fig. 270: The completed oak tree, styled on the tree pictured in Fig. 14 (in Chapter 1). The density of this tree is perfect for screening track entering a fiddle yard and is used in such a way on the diorama built in Chapter 13.

Kevin Wilson's 'O'-gauge 'Bucks Hill'. A huge amount of perspective can be created on relatively narrow baseboards. The open nature of the trees in the foreground gives way to denser foliated trees closer to the backscene, whilst the fence that curves uphill draws the eye further into the landscape. The painted backscene takes the eye even further into the distance, and by careful positioning of the trees and by using similar colours throughout the scene, a seamless transition between foreground and background is created. PAUL BAMBRICK

CHAPTER NINE

SCOTS PINE, SILVER BIRCH AND WEEPING WILLOW

The techniques used to create the oak tree demonstrated in the previous chapter can be adapted to suit any of the diverse array of broadleaf tree species. Very convincing model trees can be produced if the characteristics of a certain species of tree can be captured, for instance in the proportions and shape of the armature, and the colour and texture of the bark and the foliage.

Approximate growth heights are given for each of the tree species demonstrated in this chapter, with a conversion into 'OO' and 'O' scales. These are the maximum heights the tree species grow to, and trees should be scaled down when making trees for model railways.

Materials

- Wire
- Aluminium planting pin
- Masking tape
- Bark Powder
- Rubberized horsehair
- Paints (including orange)
- Hairspray
- Scenic scatters
- Diluted PVA glue

Tools

- Wire cutters
- Paintbrushes
- Atomizer bottle
- Scissors

Fig. 271: A natural group of Scots pine trees. Note the long, narrow, straight trunks.

SCOTS PINE

Mature Scots pine trees can attain a massive 114ft in height, which equates to an unbelievable 46cm in 'OO' and 72cm in 'O' gauge. They have a distinctive, long straight trunk that is mostly void of living side branches and can be up to 1m (40in) in diameter – that equates to 12mm (½in) in 'OO', and 21mm (⅞in) in 'O'. Often these trunks have the remains of dead branches in the form of little 'snags' of dead wood, and there is often evidence of their having lost larger branches, too. Scots pine bark is generally dark grey in colour on the lower part of the tree, yet distinctly orange on the upper trunk and branches. Scots pines are topped with a messy crown of ever-green foliage, as seen in Fig. 271.

MAKING THE ARMATURE AND BRANCHES

Take a grip of wires: for a 25cm (10in) Scots pine in 'OO', a grip of forty wires (0.7mm diameter) is ideal. As shown previously, masking tape is put round the 'base' of the trunk to hold the wires together as the styling process commences. Push a few of the central wires down towards the taped end to create a small planting pin at the bottom of the tree. Wind masking tape round the pin and pull it tightly (see Fig. 272).

In the next stage, one option is to wrap masking tape tightly round the tree's trunk, all the way up to where the first branches at the top of the tree will grow. In this demonstration however, small dead branches are positioned all round the lower trunk, so the process is slightly different.

Take a single length of wire and cut it into short lengths of approximately 30–40mm (1–1½in). Take one of the short wires and feed it part-way through the centre of the grip of wires so that it protrudes from both sides of the tree, creating a small dead branch on each side of the tree. Some of the short wires can be bent into an angular 'Z' shape, which will help stagger the positions of the branches as they rise up the trunk.

Each time a wire is added to the trunk, wrap a small piece of masking tape round the trunk, pulling it tightly to help hold the wire in place (see Fig. 273). Obviously some of the dead branches that you add to the tree can be far thicker than a single wire to give the impression that a larger bough used to grow from there. Larger branches can be added by forcing a hole into the wire trunk once it has been taped up, and inserting a real piece of dead wood into it.

Scots pines can have very randomly shaped branches growing at unusual angles in relation to their trunks, and as with most trees, no two are ever exactly the same. A look at real trees in their

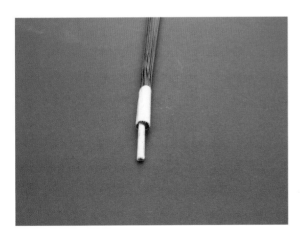

Fig. 272: Fashion a slender trunk and make a planting pin at the base.

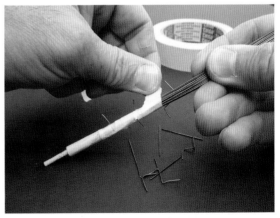

Fig. 273: Short 'snags' of deadwood are created using single wires. Masking tape keeps the trunk firm and smooth.

Fig. 274: A dead bough is made below the growing canopy. Trim the wires leaving short stubby branches.

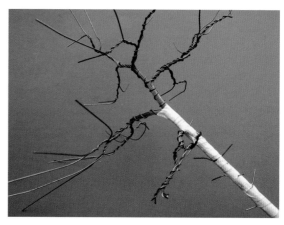

Fig. 275: The remaining wires are used to create the branches on which the foliage will rest.

natural surroundings or a search on the internet will help guide you when it comes to positioning and shaping yours.

The living branches on this example start growing from the trunk approximately two-thirds of the way up. Just below the living branches there is to be the remains of a large dead branch. To make this, take a few wires and bend them to the side. Take a single wire and wind it round the protruding wires, pulling it tight. Divide the wires into two, and continue winding the wire round one half of them.

Take another wire and wind it round the remaining half, and this time split the remaining half into two, creating a total of three branches. Cut the wires on the lowest branch using wire cutters, leaving a thick, three-pronged 'dead' branch (see Fig. 274). A small fork at the end of the thickest branch has been added.

Moving up the tree, the main branch structure can be fashioned. A Scots pine tends to have fewer yet thicker boughs than deciduous trees. Take approximately ten of the wires and create a large bough, following the techniques used for creating the boughs of the oak tree. Next take a single wire, winding it round the trunk, and move slightly further up the trunk to form a bough on the opposite side of the trunk to the first; use fewer wires on the second

bough. By using progressively fewer wires for each bough as you work up the tree the boughs higher up the trunk will be finer than the lower boughs. Work up to the top of the tree until all the original forty wires have been included in the armature (see Fig. 275).

SHAPING THE TREE

The wires can now be trimmed to length and the tree shaped. The single wires representing the fine

Fig. 276: Trim the wire to length and apply masking tape to the trunk and main branches, pulling it tight as you proceed.

branches are trimmed using wire cutters, leaving short 10–15mm (³/₈–⁵/₈in) stubs; it is these stubs that will hold the foliage in place. The trunk and main branches are tightly wound with masking tape to hide the wires wound round them (see Fig. 276). Masking tape is also useful for adding extra girth to the trunk and boughs if deemed necessary.

When all the wires have been trimmed and the masking tape applied accordingly, bend the boughs by hand, remembering that some of the boughs of Scots pine can naturally be a very unusual shape; bend all the boughs into position. Very subtle shaping and positioning of the dead branches on the trunk – and the trunk itself, too – will add to the overall look of the tree.

ADDING THE BARK

The trunk and branches can now be covered with bark. Start at the top of the tree, covering all the wires as you proceed; continue by adding the bark to the trunk. Add a little dab of bark to the snags of deadwood, just at the point where they leave the trunk. This gives the appearance that the wire is indeed thinner than the start of the branch, and implies it is dead heartwood stripped of bark (see Fig. 277). The effect is more obvious once the tree has been painted. The bark is textured with a stiff-bristled toothbrush as it dries. Run the brush vertically along the trunk and along the length of the main boughs.

Scots pine bark at the lower region of the trunk is characteristically a dark grey colour, which changes to an often surprisingly bright orange colour the further up the tree you look, where the flaking bark is younger (see Fig. 278).

The bark on the tree trunk is painted and weathered in the same way as the oak tree in the previous chapter, using a mixture of watercolour and acrylic paints. Gradually blend the two colours of paint together so there is no obvious line between the two. Use a stiff-bristled paintbrush to stipple the orange paint over the grey paint where the two join.

To give the impression of dead, weathered wood the small wire snags on the trunk and the large bough need to be carefully painted. Take a little white paint

Fig. 277: Bark is applied to the branches and trunk, and to the start of the snags. Leave the majority of the snags as bare wire.

Fig. 278: In nature, Scots pine bark changes progressively from a rugged grey in the lower parts of the tree to a flaky orange the further up the tree you look.

Fig. 279: Take your time to paint the bark and the deadwood of the tree carefully.

– emulsion paint works perfectly well for this – add a little yellow and a spot of black, and paint the 'dead' areas using a small paintbrush (*see* Fig. 279). When the deadwood has dried, 'weather' the whole armature to blend the bark and deadwood together.

Capturing these characteristics on your Scots pine trees will produce a more realistic scale model. The paint and weathering is best left to dry before the foliage canopy is added.

ADDING THE FOLIAGE

As with the hedges and some of the other trees in this book, rubberized horsehair is also a particularly good material for creating the foliage canopy of pine trees. Cut it into small pieces, then pull these apart and tease them into very open structures, large enough to cover the boughs of the tree where they are to be fixed (*see* Fig. 280). Spray the structures using dark-coloured aerosol paint to tone the fibres down a little: initially use black, then give them a light coat of an orangey-brown paint; this colour is also applied to the very tips of the branches of the armature. Spray the foliage canopy with diluted PVA and apply a sprinkling of pine scatter.

To attach the foliage pads, first carefully take up one of them and place it on the armature (*see* Fig. 281), starting on the lower boughs and working upwards towards the top of the tree, until the whole canopy is in place. Then spray the tree with dilute PVA, ensuring the entire canopy is covered with glue; this also helps the canopy adhere to the armature. A blast of hairspray will help fix the scatter to the rubberized horsehair. It is effective if another, lighter tone of scatter is added during this step as this gives the impression of fresher growth at the tips of the fine branches.

Carefully dab any glue from the trunk and boughs using a lint-free cloth, or use a damp brush to remove it. Stand the tree upright and allow it to dry, removing any further glue from the trunk as it drips down from the canopy.

REFINING THE TREE

To refine the shape and appearance of the tree, use sharp scissors to cut any of the looping fibres into two separate branches (*see* Fig. 282), as shown in the previous chapter. Scots pine trees can be fairly scruffy in appearance, so some of the longer fibres can be left hanging down or sticking out of the canopy – though bear in mind the scale of the tree, so you don't leave 'twenty foot' branches poking out from the main canopy.

Fig. 283 shows the finished tree. The Scots pine makes a very fine solitary tree, but they always look impressive when grown in small groups, sharing a common canopy which is held aloft by multiple

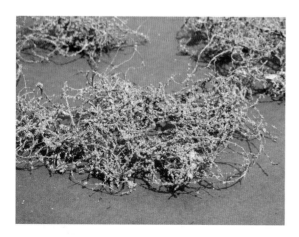

Fig. 280: Create an open-structured, slightly messy canopy.

Fig. 281: Position the canopy on the upper branches of the armature.

Fig. 282: Remove any loops of rubberized horsehair using sharp scissors.

Fig. 283: The finished Scots pine tree. Note the couple of dead branches sticking out from the upper part of the tree's foliage.

trunks. The nature of their often long, bare lower trunk makes them a good choice of tree for places on the layout where the view behind them is to be left visible.

SILVER BIRCH

Silver birch can grow up to 25m (80ft) tall – that is, 33cm (13in) in 'OO' gauge, and 52cm (20in) in 'O' – and are narrow trees on the whole. They often have a very slender trunk, rarely larger than 40cm (16in) in diameter (5mm in 'OO' and 9.5mm in 'O'), although in some birch trees it can be much wider. It is off-white in appearance and usually speckled with dark diamond-shaped markings. The colour of the bark stands out in the landscape and highlights the weathering of the trunk. Silver birch branches tend to grow upwards at an angle of approximately 45 degrees, with some having pendulous branchlets which droop down as they grow.

For scale model silver birch, and for tree species that have very thin trunks and branches, choose a wire with a smaller diameter than that used in the previous demonstrations. The trees will therefore contain a similar quantity of wires, which ultimately means they will have as many branches as trees with a thicker trunk, but the finer wires result in

Materials

- Wire
- Masking tape
- Bark Powder
- Canopy (synthetic hair)
- Paints (including white)
- Hairspray
- Scenic scatters
- Diluted PVA glue

Tools

- Wire cutters
- Paintbrushes
- Atomizer bottle
- Scissors

a thinner trunk, which is what is required for the silver birch.

The wire used here is 0.3mm in diameter and a vivid green colour, but you will see that the painting process for silver birch is different from other trees, and the colour of the wire will be covered over completely. Note that armatures built using very fine wires will inevitably have branches that are more delicate than in trees made with thicker wires.

Fig. 284: Silver birch tree: note the open structure of its canopy.

CREATING THE ARMATURE AND BRANCHES

Use a small grip of wires; here, approximately forty wires are being used, which will result in a tree with a trunk roughly 4mm in diameter. The wires are approximately 160mm (6in) in length, which will produce a small tree standing 12m (40ft) tall in 'OO' and 7m (23ft) in 'O'. The tree is constructed following the same procedures as in the demonstrations for the other trees in this book.

Create a planting pin by pulling a few wires down from the trunk, and wind a little masking tape round it. Then add a thin layer of masking tape to the lower trunk, and continue winding it right up to where the first branches start; for trees with a very slender trunk it is advisable not to coil a wire around the trunk as the tape (or layer of bark) used to hide the wire may thicken the trunk too much.

Bend a few wires to one side and fashion a long and slender side branch that 'grows' upwards at an angle of about 45 degrees. Repeat this step as you move up the tree, ideally positioning branches to the right, then left, then front, then back of the trunk as you proceed (see Fig. 285). Again, there is no definitive rule as to where branches are positioned, and often three or more may grow from the same point on the trunk; but placing them fairly equally around

the trunk results in a balanced-looking tree. Use all the wires, continuing up to the apex.

Trim all the long single wires using wire cutters – or if your wire is really fine you can use scissors – to a length of approximately 25mm (1in); bend all the tips over into a gentle arc facing outwards and downwards from the tree (see Fig. 286). Try to position the branches so each has a space below it for the pendulous canopy to droop down into, and bend them into pleasing shapes. The trunk can also

Fig. 285: Create a silver birch tree armature using fine wires.

Fig. 286: Trim the wires and bend their tips down so they point towards the ground.

Fig. 287: Coat the trunk and side branches with bark, but not the single wires.

be shaped at this stage so it isn't unnaturally straight from the lower section.

ADDING THE BARK

Apply a very thin coat of bark to the trunk and main branches, but not to the single branches, as these should be left as fine as possible (*see* Fig. 287). Allow the bark to dry

Young silver birch are often tall and narrow with a single trunk, however some mature into much wider, rounded-looking trees with a fairly thick trunk, while in others a split trunk develops, dividing low down and resulting in a tree with two or more trunks. The latter are always interesting when seen in model form.

PAINTING AND WEATHERING

Once the bark has dried, the tree armature can be painted. Unlike the other trees in this book, at this stage the armature looks very different from how it will look once it has been painted and weathered. There are certain varieties of silver birch that have very white bark, which covers even the very fine branches; however, in most the trunk and lower branches are off-white, and this blends seamlessly to much darker branch tips, which are often a deep purple/brown colour.

To paint the tree you can use either aerosol paint, acrylic, or even emulsion paint. Here, both the trunk and the fine branches have been spray-painted white (*see* Fig. 288); this is the basic undercoat on which to add the detail. Any little imperfections where paint is missing can be left, as this will add to the effect of the bark. Pure white paint applied with a brush should have a *tiny* drop of yellow paint added to it, to create an off-white colour. Allow the white paint to dry.

In its present state the tree is far too white and looks very unnatural. To start transforming it into something more like the prototype, take a dark brown paint and paint all branches that contain one or two wires. Also blend the brown paint into the thicker branches and trunk, to create something that looks like the armature in Fig. 289. The paint used for this armature is ordinary watercolour paint made by mixing some brown with a little black and purple. Painting it on to the wires in a random fashion adds more interest to the tree.

Of course the brown paint can be applied using an airbrush or aerosol as long as care is taken not to get too much on to the trunk. If this should happen, use a stiff-bristled paintbrush to return a little off-white paint to the trunk, blending it into the darker-coloured paint using the same technique as the bark on the Scots pine.

Fig. 288: The armature is given an undercoat of white or off-white paint.

Fig. 289: Look at real silver birch trees to see how their bark changes in colour the further away from the trunk it is.

In the wild, silver birch are very recognizable due to their shape and bark colour; they also display characteristic marking on their trunks, which can easily be added to our models. Observing and photographing real trees or searching the internet will give you an idea of how the markings can appear; they do vary, with some trunks being almost unmarked and very smooth, whilst others are heavily patterned and textured. They often have dark triangular or diamond-shaped markings on their trunks as well as thin horizontal lines, all of which can be easily added

before the weathering is applied. Here, the pattern is simply added to the trunk of this silver birch using a permanent marker pen with a 0.5mm tip (see Fig. 290). Allow the markings to dry if necessary.

To modify some of the starkness of the white aerosol paint the tree is weathered. Trunks can often display green, yellow, brown or even pinkish tints to the white bark areas; again, looking at the real thing will guide you. The trunk and boughs of the tree in this demonstration have been weathered using AK Interactive Slimy Grime Light weathering

Fig. 290: Use a paintbrush or fine marker pen to add the markings often seen on silver birch trunks.

Fig. 291: Weather the trunks and modify the stark whiteness of the undercoat if necessary.

Fig. 292: There is no set pattern to their markings, but silver birch are usually more marked and weathered at the base of the tree.

enamel and a dark brown watercolour paint which has been stippled on to the lower trunk area (*see* Fig. 291).

Small areas of the bark round the lower part of the tree can be carefully carved into with a sharp blade to create a rougher texture (*see* Fig. 292). Assess if any touching up with the permanent marker is required, and add further detail accordingly; then let the armature dry completely. Note that all the original white paint used to undercoat the armature has now been covered with a wash of paint or weathering material.

CREATING A WEEPING CANOPY

Stand the tree armature upright by sticking the planting pin into a block of Kingspan or polystyrene; this allows you to have both hands free for the next steps. Apply neat PVA glue to the arching branches using a small paintbrush: the amount of glue required is minimal, just enough to hold the canopy in place (*see* Fig. 293). For small trees it is possible to work quickly, covering all the branch tips with glue before adding the finer branches; however, you may choose to work on one branch at a time.

The finer branches are created using a plait of Canopy material. Take the plait in one hand, and using the thumb and forefinger of the other hand, pull a small pinch of fibres away from it. Keep the fibres

Fig. 293: To add the tree's canopy, start by applying neat PVA to the tips of the branches.

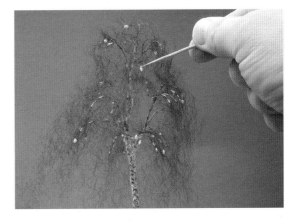

Fig. 294: Carefully add small pinches of synthetic hair to the glue, working the fibres into it with a cocktail stick.

straight, and place the top of the 'pinch' on to the glue at the end of a branch, working the fibres into it using a cocktail stick (see Fig. 294). Avoid getting any glue on your fingers, as this will cause problems with the next pinch, which will stick to them.

Start by covering the lower branches and work your way up towards the top of the tree, creating a canopy of hanging branches. The denser the canopy that is added to the tree at this stage, the denser the final foliage canopy will appear. The glue should be allowed to dry before any refining of the canopy can be done.

REFINING THE SHAPE OF THE TREE

The shape of the tree has been refined, all the overly long fibres having been trimmed off with sharp scissors; the tree at this stage is how the silver birch appears in winter. The canopy has also had a *very* light spray with a dark aerosol paint, just enough to make the fibres a little more rigid: the paint should be sprayed from at least a foot away, making sure not to ruin the work already completed on the armature. Certain varieties of silver birch have pendulous branches that actually grow down to ground level, but as most of the work for the tree in this demonstration has gone into the detail of the bark, the lower fibres have been trimmed in a way that allows the trunk to be seen (see Fig. 295).

ADDING THE FOLIAGE

To add the foliage, spray the fibres with hairspray both from above and below. Take a pinch of fine scatter and sprinkle it over the hairspray on the fibres; then take another pinch and apply it to another part of the tree. Repeat this process until all the fibres are carrying scatter. Take another pinch of scatter and sprinkle it on the inside of the fibres hanging from the bottom of the tree. A small pinch of yellow scatter is randomly added to the tree, which will give variation to the foliage colour (see Fig. 296).

To finish the tree and to ensure the scatter sticks, carefully spray the whole canopy with diluted PVA glue through an atomizer. On top of the glue apply another liberal coat of hairspray. When the tree has dried, the canopy will be surprisingly rigid and can be trimmed with scissors to refine it further (see Fig. 297).

Silver birch trees display a much larger quantity of finer branches when compared to the Scots pine tree. Their bark colour and markings make them an interesting feature on any model railway, and in the wild they tend to grow almost everywhere.

Fig. 296: Apply a light sprinkle of scatter to the fibres, though be careful not to get any on the branches or trunk.

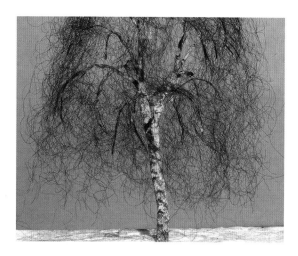

Fig. 295: Detail of the trunks and fine canopy.

Fig. 297: Use sharp scissors to remove any clumpy areas of scatter, and refine the shape of the tree.

Fig. 298: The completed tree has a nice open canopy, like the tree in Fig. 284.

WEEPING WILLOW

The weeping willow, when left untrimmed, can become a huge spreading tree growing up to 24m (80ft) tall – 32cm (12.5in) in 'OO', and 51cm (20in) in 'O' – and has a thick, strong trunk with a diameter of up to 1m (3ft) – 12mm (½in 'OO', and 21mm (¾in) in 'O'. The bark on the trunk of a mature weeping willow is rough and cork-like in appearance, and a dirty brownish yellow in colour, while the finer branches are a distinct bright yellow (see Fig. 300). These branches are pendulous, growing straight down, and from the lower boughs will grow down to ground level quite naturally. This is a very useful asset if the tree is being used to hide something behind it on the layout.

The method for creating willow trees is similar in many respects to the methods used when creating any other broadleaved tree. To avoid unnecessary repetition, refer to the demonstrations for the oak and the silver birch tree when following the instructions for the willow.

Materials

- Wire
- Aluminium planting pin
- Masking tape
- Bark Powder
- Canopy (synthetic hair)
- Paints (including yellow)
- Hairspray
- Scenic scatters
- Diluted PVA glue

Tools

- Wire cutters
- Paintbrushes
- Atomizer bottle
- Scissors

Fig. 299: Weeping willow trees are often as wide as they are tall when left to grow naturally.

Fig. 300: Whilst the trunk of the weeping willow is rugged and dark in colour, its fine branches are a very bright yellow colour.

CREATING THE ARMATURE

Creating a mature 23cm (9in) weeping willow in 'OO' uses around 100 wires (0.7mm in diameter). Bind the wires tightly together with masking tape near the bottom of the trunk, leaving approximately 20mm of wires clear of tape. Roots are optional, but thick-trunked trees can benefit visually if they are added.

Take a single wire and wind it upwards round the trunk to the point where you want the branches to be growing from. Bend some of the wires to one side, creating thick boughs with side branches as you work up the trunk. Repeat winding and splitting the wires until they have all been used.

SHAPING THE TREE

To fashion the tree into a recognizable weeping willow shape, take the individual boughs and bend them by hand: firstly bend them so they grow upwards, then bend them over so they look as if they are starting to droop. Apply this step to all the thicker boughs, then repeat the process on all the thinner side branches, bending them upwards firstly, then shaping them so they start to 'droop'.

When all the side branches have been shaped, work on all the single wires, arching them down to create the characteristic outline of the tree. During this step the tree can be bent, twisted and reshaped as much as you wish until the correct shape has been achieved.

The weeping willow often has a thick trunk, and model trees can have their trunks thickened up by applying a few layers of masking tape. Pull the tape tightly, and carefully work your way up the trunk, remembering that tree trunks are thicker at the bottom. Cover the thick boughs of the tree in the same way, but don't add any tape to the thinner branches of the tree.

ADDING THE BARK

Apply a thick coat of bark to the tree. Extra texture can be included in the bark mix by the addition of a little ballast or scatter. Start with the upper branches – though don't apply any to the single wires – and work your way down the tree.

When the trunk has been coated and the bark is still wet, stipple it using the end of a stiff brush; this gives it even more texture. Allow the armature to dry before painting it; any blobs of bark that may be on the single wire branches can be picked off by hand before painting commences. Any wires that need trimming should be tidied up at this stage before the painting process starts. The single wires can be trimmed as short as the wires on the silver birch tree, leaving only fairly short stubs, or they can be left a little longer, as they do strengthen and support the long weeping canopy.

The fine branches are given a light coat of paint. The paint can be either sprayed on using an aerosol or airbrush, or applied using a paintbrush: acrylic or emulsion paints are good for this process. The wires don't need to be totally covered in paint, just enough to blend them into the trunk. Paint and weather the trunk following the techniques outlined in Chapter 10.

ADDING THE FOLIAGE

All trees with weeping foliage can be foliated in much the same way as the silver birch. Take the canopy material and pull fine pinches from the plait. Apply a little PVA to the long single wires on the armature, and secure the canopy to the tree by ensuring the hair comes into contact with the glue.

To create the prototypical fine yellow branches, take a yellow spray paint and give all the fibres on the tree a light misting from above – though avoid getting too much paint on the main branches and trunk. When the paint dries the canopy will be rigid and much stronger.

Fig. 301: The weeping willow armature is covered with foliage in exactly the same way as that of the silver birch.

It is best to allow the paint to dry before handling the tree any further as the wet paint will cause the fibres to stick together if they are touched; however, if you are careful you can commence with the next step straight away.

Spray the fibres on the tree with hairspray, and apply the scatter as densely as is necessary to suit the tree's position on the layout. If the tree is being used to hide a certain view on the layout, then a denser application may be favourable. A lighter covering of scatter will enable the colour of the branches to show through, and allow the scene behind the tree to be seen.

Weeping willow trees are instantly recognizable due in part to their weeping growth habit and their unusually coloured bark; they don't always have branches which grow right down to the ground and they can be trimmed to any height above ground level. In the real world they are often seen in parks and gardens, and also near rivers as they have a great thirst for water and thrive in such conditions.

SUMMARY

The demonstrations in this chapter show that three very different species of tree can be created using almost identical techniques and materials. Each tree has been styled by closely copying the characteristics of the prototype tree, and in all cases the trunks and branch system have been formed using wire.

Copying the features of the trees we see in nature allows us to create the correct shape and style of the tree in model form. The wire armatures are in turn coated with bark, textured and painted to represent the species being modelled. Foliage canopies are added to the armatures in a way that makes each tree look as it would in the natural world.

Wayne Webb's N-gauge 'Dentdale', Settle and Carlisle railway. There are no hedges here, but plenty of drystone walls in evidence, which help to capture the character of the location. This landscape is built on many levels, which also adds to the realism of the scene: the terrain sweeps up from the right-hand side to the tracks, then up again to where the church is positioned. To the rear of the church a few tall trees add to the effect. ANDY YORK AND BRM MAGAZINE

CHAPTER TEN

AUTUMN AND WINTER TREES

Fig. 302: Greens, yellows, oranges and reds: autumn colours make a striking display both in nature and in model form.

AUTUMN COLOUR

Autumn is the time of the year when deciduous trees and plants lose their leaves in order to protect themselves from the cold winter months. This process, coupled with less natural sunlight, causes the leaves to lose their green appearance and gradually turn to colours ranging from bright yellow to the deepest red. Trees look spectacular in the weeks when they are losing their leaves, and when reproduced in model form can add a blast of colour to a landscape like nothing else in nature.

BLENDING AUTUMN FOLIAGE INTO THE LANDSCAPE

The processes and techniques for modelling trees with autumn foliage are almost exactly the same as for making summer trees in full leaf, though certain rules should be followed so that trees fit into the landscape without looking out of place and unrealistic. Follow all the steps in Chapter 8 with regard

to making the wire armatures, applying the bark and creating the foliage pads for the trees – but consider this for a moment: if you apply a green scatter that is exceedingly bright and gaudy to your summer trees it will make them look rather false and toy-like.

Now imagine the same principle, but this time using yellow, orange and red scatters: the problem is amplified and the resulting trees will look very toy-like indeed. Even if in nature autumn colours are sometimes incredibly bright and almost unrealistic, in model form the colours of the foliage must be made more muted in order for the trees to look realistic once they are set in the landscape. Blend different tones and colours of scatter together, as this will add to the impression of a tree that is actually turning from green to an autumn colour. Adding various tones of green scatter to a basic yellow scatter will certainly help it to blend into the landscape.

Ready-made mass-produced trees can also look unrealistic due to their bright colour, but their

Fig. 303: Autumn colours must be evident in both trees and the general scenery for the effect to work well.

appearance can be improved by the addition of scatter in more subtle colours.

A point of huge importance regarding the effect that trees will have is the model scenery in which they are placed. This landscape must have tones, colours and features that all add to the effect of an autumnal scene, and tell the story that indicates the time of year. There is little point in spending time creating realistic-looking autumnal trees that don't fit in with their surroundings. One very simple way of blending the trees into the surrounding landscape is to drop some of the scatter used to create the foliage on to the ground below and around the tree, giving the impression that it has only recently been losing leaves.

The colours used for the general grasses, weeds and hedgerows on the layout also play an important part in helping the trees blend into the scenery.

Fig. 304: Evergreen plants stand in contrast to the autumn colours of some of the trees.

Although grass can remain very vibrant in colour all year round, patches of dead grass, dead weeds and bramble stems, or other similar plants without foliage, or with foliage in a similar autumn colour, will help to link all the elements on the layout.

Evergreen trees and plants, as their name suggests, remain green all year round. The contrast between the bright yellows, oranges or reds of the trees in the landscape and the dark green of conifers, pine trees or ivy growing around tree trunks and branches, for example, can be stunning both in nature and when portrayed in model form, and serves to emphasize the autumnal appearance of some of the trees.

WINTER TREE STRUCTURE

During the winter months, after deciduous trees have lost their leaves, their branch structure, and especially the fine tracery of the smaller branches, can be clearly seen and their intricate growth pattern fully appreciated. Often tree trunks and branches can be totally covered in ivy, which may not be entirely evident whilst the tree is in leaf. Layouts set in late autumn or winter will benefit from the addition of a tree or trees that are without leaves. Winter trees

not only add interest to model railway landscapes, they also give a good indication of the season in which the model is set.

MAKING THE ARMATURE

Although it is desirable to create realistic-looking tree armatures at all times, it is essential that they are attractive and detailed when they are intended to represent trees during the winter months and will be bare of foliage. It is worth making a special effort even when the majority of the tree is to be covered in ivy. Taking photographs of trees during winter will be an invaluable resource when it comes to making your winter trees.

The armature for the tree in this demonstration has been constructed by carefully following the steps in Chapter 8, and uses both 0.7mm and 0.3mm wires (see Fig. 306). As with the other styles of tree armature in this book, masking tape is used to cover the trunk and branches. When applying the masking tape, be sure to pull it tightly to ensure a neat appearance – and remember that branches get narrower the further away they are from the trunk, so use the tape to thicken them up accordingly. As deciduous trees will not be covered in leaves during

Fig. 305: The shape, size and structure of trees in winter can be truly appreciated.

Fig. 306: This armature has been created following the techniques demonstrated in Chapter 8.

Fig. 307: Crimp the wires using long-nosed pliers.

the winter months, there is no foliage to hide any twisted wires, so masking tape is added as far along the bough as possible.

CRIMPING THE FINE BRANCHES

A technique that isn't always necessary when making summer trees but does add to the appearance of winter trees is to crimp the fine branches of the tree using long-nosed pliers or similar. This process might at first appear to be fairly time-consuming, but is well worth the effort involved.

Take one of the single wires and grip it with your thumb and forefinger at the point where it leaves the side branch. Take a pair of long-nosed pliers, and grip the wire at the end nearest your thumb. Bend the wire with the pliers to an angle of about 45 degrees, then move the pliers outwards 5mm towards the end of the branch, and bend the wire in the opposite direction, creating a kink in the branch. Continue working outwards along the branch creating a zigzag pattern as you proceed. Take the next wire and repeat the process (see Fig. 307).

It is best to work on one bough at a time, shaping all the wires on it before moving on to the next bough. With a little practice you will find that it isn't such a daunting task and can be accomplished fairly quickly.

When all the branches have been crimped, arrange them so they 'grow' outwards from the main boughs. Bending them upwards slightly also fills in the spaces between the boughs, which will help when the very fine branch structure is added later in the tree's construction.

Give the fine crimped wires a light coat of paint from an aerosol (see Fig. 308). The wires on this tree have been given a matt black undercoat and lightly sprayed using Liquitex Raw Umber 6. The coat of

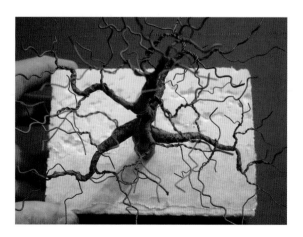

Fig. 308: Position the wires and spray them with a suitably coloured paint.

paint needn't be heavy – in fact some of the black undercoat showing through the top coat of paint adds a little variety to the branches. Of course the paint can be applied to the branches after the bark is added, but then care must be taken not to get too much on the bark covering the trunk and boughs.

ADDING THE BARK

The bark of the tree can now be applied using a fine paintbrush. Starting at the top of the tree it is important to cover all but the single wires with the bark, but not too thickly. If necessary, dilute the bark mixture slightly more than usual for the finer branches, which allows it to flow down the length of each branch. It may be necessary to go over some parts of the tree with another layer of bark to cover any bare wires that may be showing.

Note that a large area of the trunk has had fresh masking tape added to it, so that it is purposely left free of bark mixture. This will give the impression that this area of the trunk has been damaged, something which is often seen on trees. Building up the bark mixture around this area creates an interesting hollow in the trunk and gives the impression that the tree has started to heal itself (see Fig. 309). This hollow has been made at the front of the tree so it will be seen once the tree is in position on the layout.

When the trunk is weathered the damaged area will blend into the rest of the tree and look very natural.

Weather the bark using acrylic paints, watercolours or weathering pigments, or a mix of all three if you choose. Use a fine paintbrush and pay particular attention to any areas of bark that are not to be covered with ivy – around the hollow in the case of this tree and the finer branches (see Fig. 310).

The tree is given a general wash of dirty green with spots of grey, white, brown, yellow and black stippled on to the trunk in random areas, all adding to the weathering effect. Allow the paints to dry before adding the ivy.

IVY

The tree in this demonstration will have the majority of its trunk and branches covered in thick growing ivy. In model form trees like this can add a great deal of interest to the layout.

MAKING THE IVY

Canopy is pulled from the plait and teased apart in the same way as when it is used to create mounds of foliage for tree canopies; however for ivy, make mounds of hair that are fairly dense in appearance and flatter in shape. Pull enough pieces from the plait to cover the whole area on the tree you want to

Fig. 309: Create a definite edge to the damaged trunk.

Fig. 310: Once weathered the masking tape resembles old heartwood.

Fig. 311: Ivy growing round the trunk and lower branches of an old sycamore tree.

Materials

- Canopy (synthetic hair)
- Hairspray
- Scenic scatters
- Diluted PVA glue

Tools

- Scissors
- Atomizer bottle

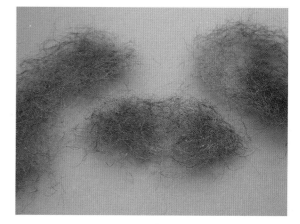

Fig. 312: Spray the fibres with a coat of paint.

cover. The tree in this demonstration is to have a very heavy coverage of ivy growing on it – but the same principles apply if you only want to cover a little of the trunk and one or two branches.

Lay the canopy material on a sheet of paper and apply a liberal spray of paint from an aerosol can from far enough away that it isn't blown from the sheet (see Fig. 312). The coat of paint doesn't need to be too heavy, and the colour chosen can be anything from a pale to mid brown to black, or a blend of colours, as can be seen here. The coat of paint is intended to strengthen the structure as much as change the colour of the fibres. It is advisable to allow the paint to dry before handling, but the following step can be undertaken with care whilst the paint is wet.

Spray a piece of canopy with a liberal amount of diluted PVA. Move the canopy to a clean piece of paper and apply a generous sprinkling of scatter; here, TREEMENDUS Pine scatter is added, highlighted with Midsummer scatter (see Fig. 313). Obviously the more scatter you apply, the thicker and denser the covering of ivy will be. Reuse the scatter which is on the paper.

Take diluted PVA and spray the ivy liberally with glue (see Fig. 314); not only will this assist in fixing the

Fig. 313: Add diluted PVA and a thick covering of dark green scatter.

Fig. 314: Soak the 'ivy' with glue and allow it to dry before handling it.

scatter to the hair fibres, it will strengthen the fibres, too. A spray of hairspray at this stage will ensure the scatter comes into contact with the glue, and will aid its adhesion. More scatter may be added at any time whilst the glue is wet.

Allow the glue to dry to be sure all the scatter is fixed in place. Be careful not to let the 'ivy' stick to the sheet of paper as it dries.

ATTACHING THE IVY TO THE TREE

Apply neat PVA glue with a paintbrush to the branches of the tree where you want the ivy to appear to be growing (see Fig. 315). It doesn't need to be applied too thickly, just enough to be able to firm the ivy into it using your fingers or a wooden skewer. You may find that adding the glue to each branch as it is about to be covered with the ivy results in a cleaner way of working. Follow the principles for adding the bark to the wire armature, starting at the top of the tree, as this allows you to hold on to the trunk if necessary whilst the glue is worked around the branches higher up the tree.

Use scissors to cut smaller pieces of the ivy away from the larger pieces you originally made, which will make it more controllable as it is applied to the armature. Obviously the glue will look unsightly at first, but will dry to a clear finish.

Take a piece of the ivy and, if necessary, tease it apart to add a little depth to it; start to work it round the branches and trunk high up the tree, pressing it into the glue as you proceed (see Fig. 316). In nature, ivy can grow clinging tightly round the branches, or sometimes it grows so thick it can almost obscure all the trunk and branches on the tree, leaving what resembles a huge mass of ivy with fine branches sticking out from it. In this demonstration the ivy

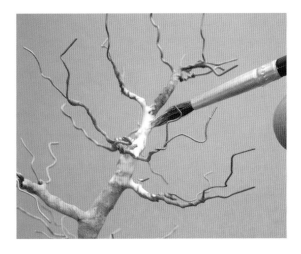

Fig. 315: Use a fine paintbrush to apply neat PVA to the branches and trunk.

Fig. 316: Carefully work little pieces of the ivy into the wet glue.

Fig. 317: Continue adding the ivy, covering the boughs and trunk as you progress.

will cling relatively tightly to the branches and trunk, allowing the shape of the tree to remain visible.

Take your time when adding the ivy to the armature. Some of the large branches on ivy-covered trees often have no ivy growing at the extremes of the boughs, and some can be left totally clear of growth. Continue adding the ivy to the upper part of the tree until the required amount has been positioned (see Fig. 317).

Next, paint some neat PVA on to the lower section of the trunk and repeat the steps above, adding ivy to the parts of the trunk where you would like to see it growing. In this demonstration the trunk will be completely covered with ivy apart from around the hollow (see Fig. 318).

Often, ivy doesn't just grow on the trees themselves: it is usually also found growing on the ground, on fences, in hedgerows and even on buildings in the immediate vicinity of the tree, and it is advisable to make more than you need for the tree during this step for use on the layout later. Rows of ivy-covered trees, whatever their size, look very impressive when placed together on a layout, and single specimen trees can be very eye-catching.

Of course the quality of the tree armature can be less than perfect if it is to be covered by ivy, but it is advisable to try to achieve a convincing armature all the same.

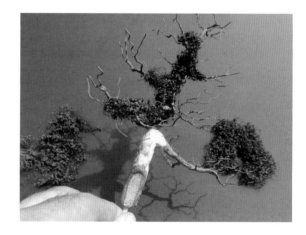

Fig. 318: Leave the damaged area of trunk clear of ivy.

FINISHING OFF

With all the ivy in place on the tree, give the whole structure a spray of hairspray, and tidy up the shape and spread of the ivy using sharp scissors, removing any long flyaway fibres (see Fig. 319). If any areas on the tree need to be thickened up a little, simply dab some neat PVA over them and trim a small piece of ivy to fit. Push the ivy into the glue to secure it (see Fig. 320).

Fig. 319: Trim the ivy where necessary, either removing it completely or thinning it out a little.

Fig. 320: The ivy can be thickened up by gluing a second layer over the original layer.

For smaller-scale trees and small trees found growing in hedgerows, another option for adding ivy to their trunks is to apply the scatter directly to the trunk itself. This is a very simple method that can yield good results. Apply neat PVA to the trunks and branches using a paintbrush, then sprinkle the scatter directly on to the glue. A misting of hairspray will help the scatter adhere to the glue.

FINE BRANCHES

Materials

- Canopy (synthetic hair)
- PVA glue
- Aerosol paints
- Hairspray

Tools

- Scissors

Fig. 321: Tease the fibres into a very open canopy, paint it and allow it to dry. The canopy was tested for size before the ivy was added to the trunk.

Although at this stage the winter tree will look acceptable as it is, it can be detailed even further with the addition of a canopy of very fine branches. To make these branches for this tree – and this is a great choice when making trees for either 'N'-, 'OO'- or 'O'-gauge model railways – again use the Canopy material that is used for the ivy.

MAKING THE FINE BRANCHES

From the plait, tease enough Canopy to cover the whole of the tree's existing branch formation. Pull the Canopy apart to create a very open-structured mound of hair. Using the same-coloured paints that were used to spray the fine wire branches on the

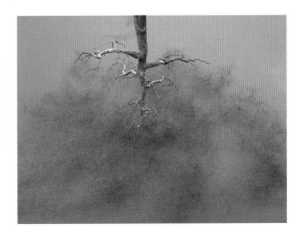

tree (black and Liquitex Raw Umber 6), lightly spray the canopy mounds from above. The tree armature is held above the painted canopy in Fig. 321 to indicate how much canopy you should create in relation to the size of the tree. The mound must be allowed to dry completely before it is handled.

ATTACHING THE BRANCHES TO THE TREE

To add the fine branch structures to the tree, carefully pick up the canopy and position it over the tree, working it into the wire branches (see Fig. 322). Spray the whole tree with hairspray and allow it to dry. What appears to be a very delicate branch structure will in fact be fairly stiff to the touch and remain durable for years. If necessary build up the tree's tracery of fine branches by adding more pieces of hair until the entire wire branch system has been covered.

Any small straggly and flyaway fibres of hair can be trimmed off using scissors as the refining process commences. If the canopy looks too dense in places or indeed all over, it can be gently teased apart further whilst on the tree and trimmed to remove some of the hair. Remember that boughs look more realistic if there are very few fine branches hanging below them, unless of course they have weeping branches, so trim and remove any fibres that hang below the main boughs (see Fig. 323). Mature trees in particular look as if their canopies are almost floating on the major boughs of the tree.

FINISHING OFF

The ivy-covered winter tree stands only 15cm (6in) tall. Note that all the fine wire branches, and the shape and colour of the ivy, are still visible through the fibres of the canopy (see Fig. 324). This is the stage in the tree's construction where a little autumn-coloured scatter would be added. First spray the canopy of the tree with hairspray, then very carefully sprinkle a *light covering* of an appropriately coloured scatter over the fibres, making absolutely sure not to get any on the ivy scatter below.

Take diluted PVA and apply a fine misting on to the scatter from a distance away that will not disturb it; then spray with hairspray, which will help hold the scatter firmly in place. Avoid handling the tree until the glue is completely dry.

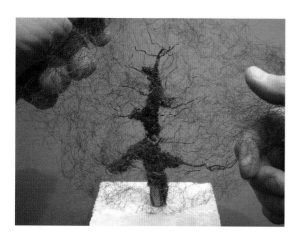

Fig 322: Apply the canopy to the armature. The structure is very open, but once the canopy is on both sides of the tree it will appear twice as dense.

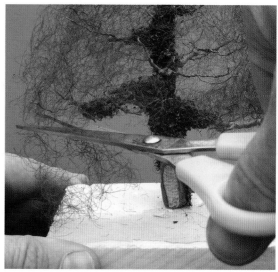

Fig. 323: Trim so that the undersides of the branches are free from canopy.

Summary

When making winter trees the time taken on detailing the wire armature before adding the bark is crucial. The detail added to the boughs and branches in the early stages of construction will be evident even when they are covered with a fine canopy of hair.

Fig. 324: The finished tree. Autumnal, or any coloured scatter could be added to the canopy at the stage.

Fig. 325: The bottom of this tree is completely covered with thick moss.

Fig. 326: Autumn colours reflected in the lake. Note the fine tracery of branches on the foreground tree.

Fig. 327: The bark of this ancient beech tree is smooth and has an almost metallic look to it.

Fig. 328: A tree with a split trunk in the open countryside. Note the lack of growth underneath its spread.

Martin Jones' EM-gauge 'Kinmundy'. A heavy frost covers the landscape in this wonderful scene, whilst the grey skies above help to enhance the impression of a cold day. The colours of the trees and groundwork can still be seen through the layer of frost, adding to the subtle effect of the scene as a whole. Trees without foliage would be well suited to scenery like this. Note, too, the weathering of the locos and rolling stock.
ANDY YORK AND BRM MAGAZINE

CHAPTER ELEVEN

FALLEN AND DEAD TREES

Fig. 329: A fallen tree in nature; there is a wealth of noteworthy detail in this photograph.

Fallen and dead trees are possibly not something you would notice on a day-to-day basis, but if you look for them you will find there are a surprisingly large number, in different sizes and various stages of decay.

The addition of a fallen or dead tree to a layout will give it extra detail and will create an interesting feature in the landscape. Trees that are blown over by the wind are often old and weak, splitting into pieces when they hit the ground, so that branches are strewn around the vicinity of the fallen tree (see Fig. 329). Even healthy trees are sometimes blown over by the wind, and these may continue growing at their newly adopted angle. Sometimes the whole rootball is lifted out of the ground, exposing the root system which is usually hidden underground (see Fig. 330).

Trees that are dying or have died more recently may remain upright and can resemble trees as they appear in the winter, with no leaves on them yet still retaining a fine tracery of branches that will eventually fall off. Other trees are reduced to nothing more than a rotten stump, which over time will vanish into the earth. Most, however, are somewhere in between, retaining only their main boughs. Scale models of dead or fallen trees will add an eye-catching feature to a layout where in contrast the other trees are healthy and in full foliage (see Fig. 331).

FALLEN TREES

This demonstration reconstructs a mostly dead tree that has been blown over, where most of the branches on the side that hit the ground have been broken off. This means it is lying flat on the ground and the grass in the field is growing around it, partly obscuring the trunk. The branches on the upper side of the trunk are designed to appear old, with most of the fine branches missing. There is also evidence of root flare at the lower trunk end, which adds to the image of the fallen tree.

Fig. 330: The exposed rootball of this tree blown over by the wind.

Fig. 331: Dead trees offer a striking contrast to the surrounding greenery.

Materials

- Wire
- Masking tape
- Bark Powder
- Paints
- Scenic scatters or static grass
- Diluted PVA glue

Tools

- Wire cutters
- Paintbrushes

CONSTRUCTING THE TREE

The tree being constructed here, when laid flat on the ground, is approximately 12cm (5in) in length. A tree of this scale will use around sixty wires, so first trim your wire to approximately 15cm (6in) lengths; the wires being used here are 0.7mm in diameter.

Take a short length of masking tape and wrap it tightly round the wires approximately 10–15mm from one end. Begin winding a single wire tightly around the main bunch of wires towards the far end of the wires. Now imagine the tree was once standing vertically, and bend fifteen or so wires upwards at the point you want the first branch to appear (see Fig. 332). Continue winding the single wire up the fifteen wires, pulling it tightly. Bend a few of the fifteen wires to one side forming a side branch, exactly as when making a tree that stands upright.

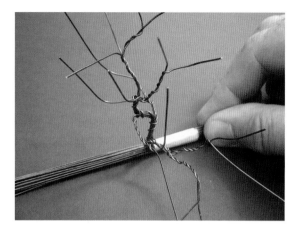

Fig. 332: Bend the wires upright to represent a small growing tree from a fallen trunk.

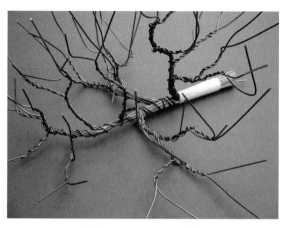

Fig. 333: Make a spreading branch system so that the tree lies flat.

Continue up the wires, splitting them and winding a single wire around them to form a branch system.

Continue using another single wire along the 'trunk' and repeat the process, but for this branch use two fewer wires than on the first branch. Consider putting the next branch to the right-hand side, forming a side branch. Wind another single wire further along the trunk and form a branch to the left-hand side; this will also ultimately give the tree side branches, which will allow it to lie flat (*see* Fig. 333). Another branch can be added to the top of the trunk again; remember to use fewer wires the further 'up' the tree you go. Proceed along the trunk until all the wires have been used.

To form a simple root system at the bottom of the tree, use your thumb, or pliers if you wish, to bend the wires beyond the masking tape outwards, forming a flare at the trunk where it once stood in the ground (*see* Fig. 334). To create a more solid-looking root system the outer wires of the trunk can be twisted together to create chunkier roots, exactly as created on trees that stand vertically.

The tree can be given a more natural look by bending the trunk and side branches (*see* Fig. 335). As you bend the side branches, keep checking that the tree will lie relatively flat once it is in position on the layout. Handmade wire tree armatures can be bent and shaped to fit any undulations in the terrain,

Fig. 334: Roots can be added to the end of the trunk.

and if their exact final position in the layout is known, they should be shaped accordingly at this stage in their construction.

REFINING THE TREE SHAPE

Take a pair of wire cutters and trim back the branches, removing most of the single wires from the tree; one or two can be left in place (*see* Fig. 336). Do not remove the single wires from the area where there is to be a little growth, as these will support the foliage canopy.

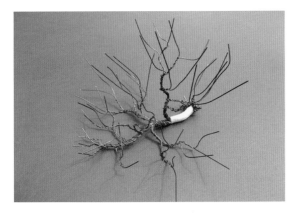

Fig. 335: Bend the wires to give the tree a more natural shape.

Fig. 336: Remove most of the single wires, leaving only short, stubby branches.

Bend all the wires so as to create what looks like a tree that was originally growing upright.

The wires that will be supporting the living canopy have been trimmed with wire cutters and crimped using pliers (see Fig. 337). Note how the bough has been shaped to look like a small tree growing upright from the horizontal trunk.

Wind masking tape round the trunk and boughs to hide the wires wound round them; pull the tape tightly, using more than one layer if necessary. Cover the trunk and main branches, and readjust the shape of the tree to show it at its best. A couple of small branches have been made using the offcut wires; they will be covered with bark like the rest of the tree, and used as detail in the groundwork round it (see Fig. 338).

ADDING THE BARK

Bark is applied to the trunk using a paintbrush in exactly the same way as it is applied to upright trees. Apply it to the trunk nice and thickly. Leaving small areas of the masking tape showing through the bark layer gives the impression of small hollows in the tree where the bark is missing, as demonstrated on the ivy-covered winter tree in the previous chapter.

Diluting the bark a little more and allowing it to run down the tips of the 'dead' branches will give the

Fig. 337: The wires on the growing part of the tree can be shaped and crimped.

Fig. 338: Cover the trunk and branches with masking tape. Prepare a couple of small boughs that will lie next to the tree.

impression of smooth, dead heartwood that has lost its bark (see Fig. 339).

The barked areas (not the deadwood branches) can be textured by lightly dragging a stiff-bristled paintbrush over the trunk and branches once the bark is almost dry (see Fig. 340). Allow the bark to dry completely before painting it.

PAINTING THE TREE

The tree can be painted using watercolour, acrylics or oil-based paints. The areas of tree that retain bark are painted using a dark grey/brown watercolour with small dabs of green, brown and white dabbed on to it whilst the grey paint is still wet. Any dabs of paint will find their own way into all the small fissures in the bark.

The dead wood of the tree is painted to represent dry dead wood using white emulsion paint with a spot of yellow and black paint added to it. Add a little extra white paint to parts of the dead wood to slightly vary the individual branches. Bark will appear much darker when the paint is wet, and the true colour will not be apparent until it has dried.

In addition to the paint on the bark a diluted wash of AK Interactive Slimy Grime Light weathering enamel has been painted over the whole tree (see Fig. 341).

MAKING THE CANOPY

The canopy for the tree is made using synthetic hair which is pulled from the plait and teased apart to form an open and airy structure. To recap, the hair is sprayed with a dark-coloured paint to strengthen it a little. Hairspray is applied to the hair, and a fine scatter is lightly sprinkled on whilst the hairspray is still wet. Carefully put the canopy on to the tree armature and spray with diluted PVA.

Once dry, the canopy is glued to the armature and the scatter securely fixed to the synthetic hair (see Fig. 342). Scissors are used to neaten the canopy by removing any long fibres and cutting any fibres which form loops, in the same way as previous demonstrations when the rubberized horsehair canopies were refined.

Fig. 339: Use runny bark to cover the deadwood parts of the tree.

Fig. 340: The bark on the tree can be textured as it dries using a stiff paintbrush.

Fig. 341: Paint and weather the bark.

Fig. 342: A delicate canopy is added to the live portion of the tree.

ROOTBALLS

Creating a detailed rootball which can be fixed to the base of a mass-produced tree is a very simple way to give it some individuality. Sometimes when trees fall they are seen to have very shallow roots, and the amount of earth brought up with the rootball is minimal. Others fall revealing a deep 'scoop' of earth, full of roots, soil and stones and measuring many feet across. Mass-produced model trees can also be improved with the addition of bark over their plastic trunks, and a very light secondary coating of scatter to add contrast to their foliage.

MAKING THE ROOTBALL

To create the detailed rootball, take a piece of Kingspan, polystyrene or compressed paper ceiling tile, and using a sharp blade, cut out a 'bowl'-shaped section which is flat on the top and rounded beneath (*see* Fig. 343). Make the segment circular or oval in shape, but trim a piece from one edge to leave a flat side: this side will be laid flat on the surface of the groundwork. Ideally, for the best effect, a hollow the corresponding shape and size of the rootball can be removed from the baseboard where the tree is to be fixed, but as these holes in nature often become filled with all kinds of natural debris over time, it

Materials

- Kingspan/polystyrene
- Black/dark brown paint
- Hairspray
- Scenic scatters/stones
- PVA glue
- Real roots

Tools

- Sharp blade
- Cocktail stick/thin nail
- Paintbrush

isn't absolutely critical to do this. Make a hole in the top side of the segment where the tree will be positioned.

The rootball is given an undercoat of paint to hide the unrealistic colour of the base material. The paint, ideally brown or even black, can be applied by brush or sprayed on using an aerosol or airbrush (*see* Fig. 344). Allow the paint to dry.

Paint the underside of the rootball with PVA, add some small stones, the same colour as can be seen

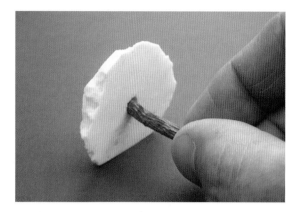

Fig. 343: Kingspan is carved into a small 'scoop' shape.

Fig. 344: Give the rootball an undercoat of black or brown paint.

Fig. 345: The rootball is coated with PVA and small stones are added to the base. A coat of Earth Powder is also applied to the glue.

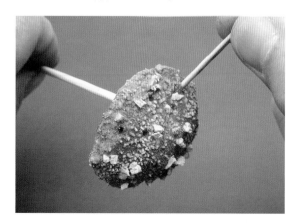

Fig. 346: Small holes are made in the base of the rootball using a cocktail stick.

elsewhere in the vicinity of the tree, and sprinkle it with an appropriately coloured Earth Powder or fine scatter, again the same colour as the soil in the immediate area around the tree (see Fig. 345). Allow the glue to dry.

ROOTS FOR THE ROOTBALL

When the rootball has dried and the soil and stones are fixed to it, take a pointed tool – a thick piece of wire, small nail or cocktail stick is ideal – and make some holes in its base (see Fig. 346). A root will be glued into each hole, so make as many holes as you want there to be roots, and place them in random positions.

For the roots, the best material to use by far are tiny pieces of real root. These can be gathered by pulling up very young saplings and trimming the very fine roots from them, or by trimming them from fallen trees. They become very strong once they have dried, and not brittle as you might imagine.

Dip the tips of the roots into glue and insert them into the holes you have made (see Fig. 347). A little Earth Powder or scatter can be added round the hole to fill any gap if required.

ADDING THE TREE

A small tree is added to the rootball, held in place with superglue; in this case it is a mass-produced fir tree from Noch. It has had its trunk replaced with a

Fig. 347: The tips of natural roots are dipped into glue and inserted into the holes.

Fig. 348: A fir tree is glued into the top of the rootball. It has had a little orange scatter added.

small length of natural branch, and brown and orange scatter has been added over the original scatter to give it the look of a tree that is dying (see Fig. 348). The top side of the rootball can be detailed later to ensure it blends in well with its surroundings.

FINAL DETAILS

The finished rootball gives a hint of what lies beneath the surface of the scenery. The roots have been trimmed to a scale of approximately 60–90cm (2–3ft) in 'OO'. A light sprinkling of scatter has also been added to some of the roots to give the impression of moss growing on them: spray the rootball with a light misting of diluted PVA and carefully apply the scatter. A few Raw Grass fibres complete the rootball. The tree itself has had its colour toned down by spraying over it with a light brown paint; this gives an impression of its foliage drying out (see Fig. 349).

Fig. 349: The tree has been toned down with aerosol paint to give it a dried-out look.

DEAD TREES

Materials

- Wire
- Aluminium planting pin
- Masking tape
- Bark Powder
- Paints

Tools

- Wire cutters
- Paintbrushes

In this demonstration a 23cm (9in) tall tree is made using wire with a 1mm diameter. Due to the lack of fine branches, dead trees such as this are quick and easy to make. As the tree is to be placed on the embankment towards the rear of the diorama built in Chapter 13, there is no need to create any root system, as the base of its trunk will be hidden in undergrowth. As with the other trees in this book, a small planting pin is made at the bottom of the trunk, to fix it into the embankment.

MAKING THE TREE

Take enough wires to create a trunk with the appropriate girth, add masking tape to the bottom of the trunk, and wind a single wire upwards round the trunk. Trees growing closely together often have few or no branches growing from their lower trunk due to the lack of light the tree receives beneath its canopy, so the dead branches of this particular tree will start about two-thirds of the way up the trunk (approximately 15cm (6in) up).

Bend ten or so wires to one side at the point where you want the first branch. Twist the wires and divide them into two branches, and twist these together. Split the wires again and twist them, creating thick boughs. Repeat this step until all the wires have been included in the branch system.

Trim most of the single wires off the tree using wire cutters; this will leave thick side branches with little taper, creating the look of branches that have snapped and fallen from the tree (see Fig. 351). Dead

Fig. 350: The basic shape of a dead tree is formed using wire.

Fig. 351: Use wire cutters to remove most of the length from the branches, leaving short stubs.

Fig. 352: Cover the trunk and branches with masking tape; on this occasion run the tape vertically up the trunk.

Fig. 353: Apply the bark in the usual way but leave a large section of masking tape clear towards the front of the tree.

trees can retain many branches like this, and it is up to you how many you create.

The wire winding up the trunk is carefully snipped at the point it reaches the first bough and removed from the trunk. This will make for a trunk with a smoother appearance, which will serve you well when creating the look of the heartwood exposed where the bark is missing.

Masking tape is added to the branches to hide the twisted wire and to thicken them up where necessary. Masking tape is also added to the lower trunk, but this time as well as being wound round the trunk in the way shown in the previous demonstrations, it is also added to the front of the trunk vertically, running up the length of the tree (see Fig. 352). As with the ivy-covered tree, some of the tape will not be covered with bark, therefore adding the tape vertically ensures that any overlapping tape will not be seen once the tree is finished.

ADDING THE BARK

Bark is applied thickly to the side branches using a paintbrush; use two coats if required to thicken them up and hide the wires. Towards the front of the trunk the dead heartwood is left free of bark (see Fig. 353); the join between the bark and the heartwood can be given a definite edge by building up the edge of the bark in layers. When the bark is almost dry, drag a stiff-bristled paintbrush down the length of the trunk and boughs to add some detail and texture. Allow it to dry completely before painting.

PAINTING AND WEATHERING THE TREE

The bark of dead trees often takes on a grey appearance, and tends to flake off after a time, due to its drying out and weathering. The exposed heartwood also tends to change to a grey colour with streaks of white, yellow and black evident, and should be painted accordingly. As the bark and heartwood generally weather together they often eventually end up displaying very similar colours, as can be seen in Fig. 354.

The barked and heartwood areas of the tree are painted with either watercolour or acrylic paints. Mix a medium-coloured grey paint and give the whole tree a light wash with it. Whilst the paint is still wet, use a stiff-bristled paintbrush to dab on thin washes of white, brown, black and yellow watercolour paints.

Fig. 354: Note the colour and textures visible on this dead tree.

Fig. 355: Paint and weather the armature.

Fig. 356: The completed dead tree.

White emulsion paint is used as the base colour for the heartwood of the tree. Take a drop of white paint and mix into it some black and yellow water-colour paints, just enough to take the starkness of the white away. Use a fine paintbrush to work the emulsion into the heartwood areas of the tree; whilst the paint is wet it can be detailed with streaks of black, yellow and white paints.

When the paint has dried, the tree can be weathered using diluted acrylic paints or weathering products; this helps age the tree and brings the two contrasting textures together, forming a natural-looking dead tree (*see* Fig. 355). In the natural world, dead trees, like all other trees, look different depending on the weather conditions, and appear darker when their bark is wet.

Fig. 356 shows the size and scale of the finished tree, whilst Fig. 357 allows the detail present on the trunk to be seen. Compare the colours and the texture of the bark of the model to the prototype. The model tree has been weathered with a little more green than the prototype tree, allowing it to blend in well with its eventual place at the rear of the layout. Because of its position at the rear of the diorama it has been created with all the branches to the sides or front, in the 'half-relief' style.

Fig. 357: The detail to the bark is created by the use of paints and weathering enamels.

Fig. 358: Note how the dead heartwood weathers to the same colour as the rest of the tree over time.

Fig. 359: Close-up of a hollow trunk and dead heartwood on an old oak tree.

Fig. 360: The trunk of this fallen tree is completely obscured by long grass, leaving only the dead branches visible.

Pendon Museum's EM gauge 'Midland and South Western Junction Railway'. This photograph shows the continuity of the colours and features in the landscape. Note how the pale colour of the lanes and tracks within the scene are all the same colour, implying they are indeed part of the same natural landscape.
ANDY YORK AND BRM MAGAZINE

CHAPTER TWELVE

HALF-RELIEF TREES

Fig. 361: The row of trees at the rear of the track at Irwell Vale is a perfect backdrop for the trains.

Half-relief (or low-relief) trees, as the name suggests, are trees constructed in such a manner that they are very shallow in depth from front to back. They are actually made using exactly the same materials, methods and principles as full-relief trees, and are initially very similar in construction to the fallen tree demonstrated in Chapter 11.

Trees constructed in half relief are a useful option to the railway modeller, especially where space is limited on the layout. Having a flat back but a three-dimensional front, they can be made to fit flush with the backscene or other flat surfaces on the layout, such as buildings or viaducts.

The half-relief trees made in this demonstration will be placed on the embankment to the rear of the layout. This particular row of trees will be fairly dense in appearance, like the ones in the field-trip photographs (*see* Figs 361 and 362), and will fill the whole of the backscene from left to right to create a spectacular backdrop for the trains.

Fig. 362: A great variation in colour and texture is evident on the embankment.

HALF-RELIEF ARMATURES

Materials

- Wire
- Masking tape
- Bark Powder
- Paints
- Hairspray
- Rubberized horsehair/canopy (synthetic hair)
- Scenic scatters, assorted colours and textures
- Diluted PVA glue

Tools

- Wire cutters
- Paintbrushes

MAKING THE ARMATURES

The row of trees will consist of seven groups of wires standing approximately 15–20cm (6–8in) in height (see Fig. 363), which equates to trees of approximately 11–15m (37–50ft) in height, with almost no trunk showing at ground level. Each tree will contain approximately forty to sixty wires of 1mm diameter. As the row of trees is to be fairly dense the armatures don't need to be constructed with the greatest detail or intricate branch systems; the important thing is that there are enough wires to hold the canopy in place. There are no visible root systems on the trees being modelled, so in this instance there is no need to bend up any wires to create roots.

Pull a few wires out from the main bunch to create planting pins, and wrap masking tape tightly around the pins and the lower trunks. Note that although the back of the tree is designed to be flat and bare of branches, there is no need for the actual trunk of the tree to have a flat back too.

MAKING THE BRANCHES

The trees on the embankment close to Irwell Vale have branches that start at almost ground level, so there is very little space between the foliage on the embankment and the leaves on the lower branches; with this in mind, the branches of these trees will start at the lowest point on the trunk (see Fig. 364). Bend a few wires outwards and downwards away from the main bunch: these wires will form the

Fig. 363: Seven groups of wires ranging from 15–20cm (6–8in) in length are prepared for the row of half-relief trees.

Fig. 364: The first branches are growing very low down on the trunks in the prototype photograph, hiding the top of the embankment.

lowest branch of the tree. This technique applies to all the trees on this embankment, but if your half-relief trees are to have visible trunks, then wind a single wire around the 'trunk' to the point where you want to place the lowest branch.

The fact that there are few, if any, gaps through the trees on the prototype embankment can be used to our advantage, as it will help to screen the space at the back of the baseboard. If you choose to erect a painted or pre-printed backscene to your layout, which is always a good idea as they do enhance the scenery on the baseboard, then any gaps in the foliage will show the hillside or sky behind it, adding to the effect of the trees.

The lowest branch of the tree is formed by winding the wires around each other and separating them as work progresses (see Fig. 365), until they have all been incorporated into the branch. If your terrain is already in situ, and the half-relief trees you are making are to sit on top of a small embankment with their branches starting at almost ground level, like the trees in this demonstration, it is good practice to give them a trial run on the embankment to make sure that the angle of the lowest branch is correct and will lie almost at ground level once it is planted. Of course wire tree armatures are flexible even when completed, and can be manipulated to

fit their positions on the layout prior to adding the bark. The groundwork foliage on the embankment can also be built up if necessary, to meet the foliage on the trees.

As in the previous demonstrations, be sure to use fewer wires per branch the further up the tree you go, as branches tend to get thinner the further up the tree they are. This is less important on trees that will be covered in thick foliage, as the side branches will probably not be seen, but this is a good practice to adopt all the same, ensuring that any small gaps in the foliage don't reveal overly heavy branches at the tops of the trees.

Continue by winding the wires up the trunk, forming side branches as you proceed. The lowest branch protrudes directly from the front of the trunk and hangs down slightly to follow the contour of the embankment. The next two branches are slightly further up the trunk, one to the left and the other to the right. As more wires are wound together, more branches are created on the armature, the fourth branch sticking straight out, the fifth to the left, and the sixth to the right. This pattern is continued until all the wires have been used (see Fig. 366).

Fig. 366 also shows the tree lying on a flat surface, and demonstrates how it will stand flush to the backscene once it is positioned on the layout. It is

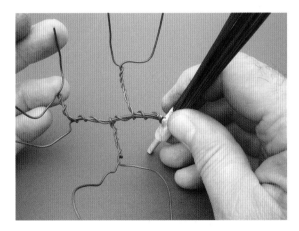

Fig. 365: Create the first branches low down on the trunks.

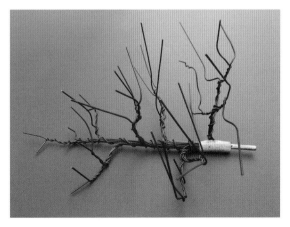

Fig. 366: Continue winding the wires until they have all been used in the armature. Note how similar the tree is at this stage to the fallen tree in the previous chapter.

Fig. 367: Trim the wires to about 20mm (¾in) in length.

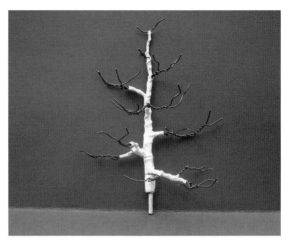

Fig. 368: Cover the wires with masking tape.

Fig. 369: The row of trees is very dense but a little daylight does show through them.

important that all the boughs and side branches are bent forwards so as to leave the back of the tree clear.

All the single wires on the tree, which form the finest branches, are trimmed with wire cutters to leave short 15–20mm stubs (see Fig. 367). The stubs can be crimped using pliers to remove the straightness from the wires.

The trunk and main branches are given a thin dressing of masking tape to conceal the wires wound round them (see Fig. 368). Although the majority of the branches and trunk won't be seen through the dense foliage, it is still advisable to add the tape to hide any wound wires that may be visible through small gaps in the foliage.

The shape of the tree can be refined as required. Bend all the main branches and stubs forwards, keeping the back of the tree flat. The boughs and trunks can also be shaped by bending them by hand, just enough to modify any straight lines.

CONSTRUCTION PROCEDURE

When making a quantity of tree armatures it is best to make them in stages, completing the basic armatures for all the trees first, then adding the tape, and then applying the bark to them all, as opposed to making one complete tree from start to finish and having to repeat the process as many times as the number of trees required.

Fig. 370 shows seven half-relief wire armatures 150–200mm in height (6–8in approximately) and 125–150mm (5–6in approximately) in width. All seven trees have had the single wires trimmed leaving only short stubs, they have been bent into pleasing shapes, and covered with masking tape. Note how flat they lie on the table top.

The finer wires of the armatures have been sprayed with aerosol paint, mainly to hide the shiny metal tips that show where the wires have been snipped. The remainder of the branches and trunks have had a coat of bark applied to them: be sure to cover all the branches and trunks, both front and back, following the techniques demonstrated in the previous chapters. Allow the bark to dry over twenty-four hours, by which time the trees can be painted and lightly weathered using watercolours and acrylic paints (see Fig. 371).

Most half-relief trees can have the fibres for their canopies added to them whilst they are laid on their backs. However, with trees such as the weeping willow, which has branches that hang down, it is best to apply their foliage whilst the armatures are fixed in an upright position.

POSITIONING THE TREES

To position the trees, glue the armature planting pins into holes which have been drilled into a 1m (3ft) length of timber. Like this, the trees are in the positions they will be in on the layout, and are much easier to work on when they are held securely in place; furthermore the continuity of the foliage when the trees are worked on as a complete row will ultimately be more realistic, too. Although the trees are fairly evenly spaced, avoid placing them exactly the same distances apart. Note too that the dead tree, made in the previous chapter, has been added

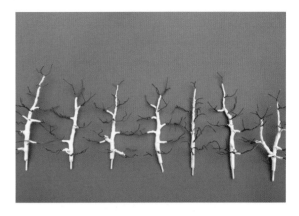

Fig. 370: It is advisable to work on all the armatures in stages rather than build one tree at a time.

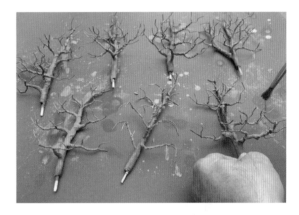

Fig. 371: Paint and weather all the armatures.

Fig. 372: The armatures are fixed into a length of timber in their final positions. Note that the dead tree demonstrated in the previous chapter has been included in the row.

to the row, third from the left (see Fig. 372). When the trees are complete, the length of timber they are glued into will be fixed to the baseboard. The front of the timber will be hidden by a small embankment which will come down at an angle of approximately 45 degrees and finish just behind the railway track.

ADDING THE FOLIAGE

The trees on the embankment at Irwell Vale are a mixture of species and therefore display an assorted blend of colours and textures in their foliage. The trees for the model have had a layer of rubberized horsehair added to them. One of the trees has had a thin layer of synthetic hair carefully laid over the rubberized horsehair to give it a much finer branch structure, and one of the trees has had no fibres added as yet because it will be given hanging branches once the other trees have been foliated.

Building Groups of Trees

Large forests, small copses and groups of even two or three trees can be built as a single structure sharing a common canopy held aloft by a number of trunks and branches. The wire armature for this type of feature can be constructed in a way that combines all the individual trees into one single wire framework. Building groups of trees using this method makes it appear as though the trees have grown together and are not a group of single trees that have been placed together. In the case of forests and small copses, numerous trunks void of branches can be added among the actual tree armatures to give the impression of there being far more individual trees than there actually are.

Fig. 373: Although this natural row of trees is not to the rear of the track, it is a perfect reference for modelling half-relief trees.

The horsehair has been given a couple of light coats of paint, firstly black, followed by mid brown. Note in Fig. 374 that the dead tree has been masked off using paper, to ensure that no paint gets on to its trunk or branches. If the paint is applied with care and not sprayed heavily into the fibres, the armatures, which are already weathered, will not be affected.

There is little need to repeat the whole process involved with adding the trees' foliage: suffice it to say that both the rubberized horsehair and synthetic hair are teased apart to form the basic tree shape. Both can be given a light coat of aerosol paint, ideally one that matches the colour of the armatures – although in this demonstration they are added to the tree armatures unpainted, and given a light coat of paint once they are on the tree: the rubberized horsehair benefits from the paint in so much as it tones down the fibres a little, and the synthetic hair is strengthened by the paint resulting in a more robust canopy.

Next the fibres are sprayed with hairspray, and scatters are added: use an overall base colour of scatter, and a different colour for each species of tree being modelled – but also use additional sprinklings of other colours and granule sizes to add highlights to the tree canopies (see Fig. 375). Moreover a common colour of very fine scatter added to all the trees in the row will bring continuity to the effect of the layout. The trees are then finished off with a liberal spraying of diluted PVA glue applied through an atomizer.

Note that various effects can be achieved according to how each material is prepared before adding the scatter: for example, the more the fibres are teased apart, the more open the finished tree will look. Some foliage looks very rounded and full, whereas some trees have pendulous branches hanging from their wire armature. For pendulous branches the synthetic hair is pulled from its plait and left to hang down, as opposed to being shaped into rounded foliage pads. Referring to previous demonstrations will guide you through the steps required for each effect.

REFINING THE TREES

Once they have dried completely, the trees are tidied up in the usual way. Take a pair of sharp scissors and trim away any unwanted fibres that spoil the look of the trees; be especially vigilant with regard to any over-long fibres, and any that form unrealistic-looking loops in the canopy (see Fig. 376). Small areas

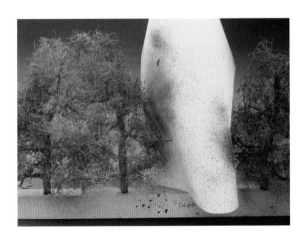

Fig. 374: Rubberized horsehair is added to the armatures and lightly painted to tone down the fibres. Note that the dead tree armature has been masked off using a sheet of paper.

Fig. 375: Cover the fibres with a mixture of scatters to add variety to the tree canopies.

Fig. 376: Tidy up the trees using sharp scissors.

Fig. 377: Remove any strands that appear too long. These trees are at the rear of the scene and should be trimmed fairly neatly.

of the foliage can be thinned out completely to reveal the wire armature behind it.

Remove all the long fibres from the tops of the trees, too (see Fig. 377). This row of trees is to be placed at the rear of the scene and will therefore be furthest away from the viewer: trimming them neatly will help give the impression that they are further away.

The bottoms of the trees will also benefit from being trimmed, using sharp scissors. Keep the branches of the lower sections of the trees in line with the top of the embankment as in the prototype photographs (see Fig. 378), though avoid making a perfectly straight line along the whole row of trees.

Continue working along the row, trimming all the unwanted fibres and refining the shape of the trees, creating little gaps in the foliage which allow the backscene to show through (see Fig. 379). More scatter can be added to any areas on the trees that require it: spray a little diluted PVA on to the fibres and sprinkle on the relevant colour.

The main difference in the refinement of half-relief trees is that not only are the fronts of the trees refined in the usual way, but the backs of the trees must be trimmed so they are relatively flat, so they sit flush with the backscene or buildings they are to be placed in front of. It may be necessary to create more pieces of canopy to fill any obvious gaps between the back of the trees and the surface

Fig. 378: The bottom of the canopy is trimmed so it will sit flush with the top of the embankment.

Fig. 379: Open up small areas of the canopy to reveal some of the trunks and branches; this will allow some of the printed backscene to be visible, too.

Tip

It is advisable to check the depth of half-relief trees that are likely to come into close proximity to the track on the layout from time to time throughout their construction. Checking them before adding any foliage allows for them to be trimmed even further back with wire cutters if necessary. Check them again when the foliage has been added and trim them back accordingly where necessary.

Trees can also be made with just a section, a quarter, for example, of branches missing as opposed to a complete half. Although not strictly 'half-relief', these trees are fashioned in a very similar way in that they are made to fit into a small or awkward area on the layout, and are very useful where unsightly angled corners are unavoidable. These may arise because of something physical on the layout such as a building, or something less attractive, such as a part of the room where the layout is built, a chimney breast for example, which may interfere with the baseboard of a layout that runs round the walls.

External and internal angles can be disguised on the layout using tree armatures which are created to fit into the offending area. External right-angles can be hidden by trees that have a quarter of their trunk clear from branches, and internal angles by trees that are no more than a quarter of a full tree. Tree armatures built to fit round corners are made in exactly the same way as other tree armatures, except that they have a section of trunk which is clear of branches.

behind them; it is best to do this once the trees are in position on the layout.

THE COMPLETED ROW

In Fig. 380 the completed row of trees is positioned in front of a scenic backscene. Light between the back of the trees and the backscene adds to the openness of the trees, and the distant view of the printed backscene is visible through the trees.

In Fig. 381, however, the trees have been positioned closer to the backscene: note how they sit almost flush with the landscape image behind them. This lets in less light between the two and makes the trees appear much denser than in the previous image. The gaps on the groundwork between the tree and the embankment will be filled with vegetation and other ground-covering materials once the trees are securely in place on the layout.

Fig. 380: 'A trick of the light': light between the backscene and the trees makes them appear open in structure.

Fig. 381: The closer the trees are placed to the backscene, the denser they appear. They resemble the prototype more in this photograph.

Fig. 382: The final photograph shows perfectly the impression that the row of trees will make on our layout.

BELOW: John Farmer's P4 'Netherhope'. In this scene there is a stark difference between the slightly overgrown 'railway' side of the fence, and the short-grass field containing small yellow and white flowers in front of it. The trees to the rear of the scene provide a little height in the landscape. Note, too, that the fence posts are not all uniformly upright and spaced. ANDY YORK AND BRM MAGAZINE

CHAPTER THIRTEEN

CREATING A LANDSCAPE

During the course of this chapter many of the techniques and individual elements that have been demonstrated throughout the book are brought together in the creation of a scale model landscape. The landscape is based on the reference photographs shown in Chapter I and elsewhere in the book. The intention is not to copy one particular scene, but to use the colours, textures and features shown in the reference photographs to achieve a faithful representation of the landscape surrounding Irwell Vale Halt. The baseboard for the diorama is a piece of chipboard measuring 90 × 60cm (3 × 2ft).

It is important to stress at this stage that the photographs you will be working from are almost certainly going to be viewed on a computer screen and will therefore be far larger in size than the photographs that appear in a printed book; you will also be able to zoom in on certain features within the photographs. Therefore although some of the references made to the details in the field trip and other photographs may not be clearly evident in the photographs in this book, they will be easily seen on a computer screen.

THE BACKGROUND

Fig. 383 captures perfectly how the landscape through which the trains run will look. In the background tall trees grow tightly together to form a very dense backdrop to the fields in the foreground; their colours are varied, but are generally darker than the fields in the foreground. The colour variation of the grasses in the field in front of the dark-coloured trees also adds to the appearance of the scene. Around the shorter, recently cut grass there is a strip of longer, darker grass running around the perimeter of the field; the longer grass contains a fair number of tiny yellow flowers and the occasional taller weed.

Fig. 383: Note the colour difference in the recently mown field compared to the grass remaining on its periphery.

Fig. 384: The wealth of information in this prototype photograph is invaluable.

THE FOREGROUND

Fig. 384 captures some of the natural elements that will be included on the embankment and in the foreground of the diorama. The way in which all the different varieties of plant life grow together to form a harmonious living blanket covering the embankment is a pleasure to emulate on our model railways. Also growing on the embankment in front of the track are very dense trees, and open-structured ones.

In front of the embankment is a narrow strip of paddock enclosed by a simple fence, with both short grass and longer tufts of grasses growing in it; these appear blended together with buttercups, docks, nettles and small clumps of dead grass heads.

THE DESIGN

The line drawing in Fig. 385 is a rough sketch of the model landscape based on the photographs above and in Chapter 1. It is always a good idea to sketch out the scene you wish to create and to include

all the elements you are planning to fit into it. The drawing includes tall trees to the rear of the scene, with the railway line on a small embankment running in front of them. The wall in the field trip photos which runs in front of the railway line has been replaced by simple fence posts, though these are almost hidden by the vast mix of plants on the lower part of the embankment. There is a large hedgerow tree on the embankment just behind the fence to the right of the scene.

A path runs in front of the left-hand side of the embankment and disappears underneath the track via an underpass, just like the path near Irwell Vale. To the front of the path there is a simple fence of wooden posts and wire. In front of the fence there is an overgrown patch of ground full of all kinds of plants, and a large oak tree accompanied by a smaller silver birch.

The two fields in front of the lower embankment are very different in appearance; they are separated by a hedge, a dry gully, and a row of old-looking fence posts. The hedge is well trimmed on the field side, but is in a more overgrown state around the outside where it blends into the surrounding groundwork.

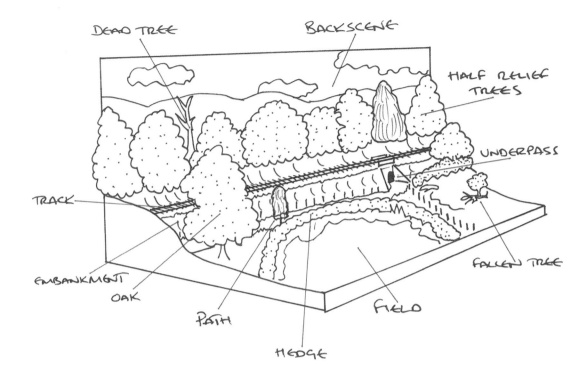

DEAD TREE

BACKSCENE

HALF RELIEF TREES

UNDERPASS

TRACK

FALLEN TREE

EMBANKMENT

OAK

PATH

FIELD

HEDGE

Fig. 385: Line drawing showing the basic plans for the diorama. In your own project, include as much detail in the drawing as possible and use it as a reference.

CONSTRUCTING THE LANDSCAPE

A bare, undulating terrain has been created based on the photographs in Chapter 1 and the accompanying line drawing.

The height of the rear embankment on which the half-relief trees will be growing is approximately 10cm (4in), and has been calculated so as not to interfere with the trains running on the embankment below them. The timber that the row of half-relief trees is attached to will simply be glued or screwed to the top of the baseboard.

Polystyrene or Kingspan are both ideal materials for creating undulations in a landscape, but as this one is fairly flat, compressed paper ceiling tiles are used to build up the embankment and field heights. The embankment on which the track will be laid

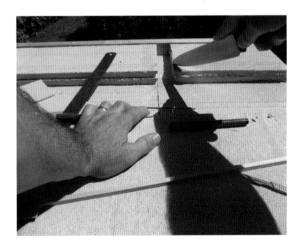

Fig. 386: The first step is to create a physical terrain through where your trains can run. Chicken wire, timber, card, polystyrene and others, are all useful materials.

Materials

- Ceiling tiles (or polystyrene or Kingspan)
- Thick card (or hardboard)
- Cocktail sticks
- Neat PVA glue
- Diluted PVA glue: three parts water to one of PVA
- Cement/plaster
- Matt brown emulsion paint
- Hairspray
- Scenic modelling materials

Tools

- Ruler
- Scalpel or craft knife
- Kitchen knife or saw
- Paintbrushes
- Scissors
- Comb or brush
- Wooden skewer
- Static grass applicator
- Plastic bottle with nozzle and atomizer

Fig. 387: The undercoated underpass in place in the embankment.

has been shaped at the front to an angle of approximately 45 degrees from the track height to the path and fields below.

THE UNDERPASS

A small underpass has been handmade using 3mm thick card and embossed plastic stone sheet, and fixed into the embankment; of course these can be bought ready to use, but they are relatively easy to make. To create a simple underpass like the one used here, first remove a section of the embankment using a large kitchen knife or saw (see Fig. 386 on previous page). Next take a sheet of thick card or hardboard, and measure and trim two pieces for the inner walls, and a third piece that will sit on top of them, like a flat roof; make sure the top of the card/board sits flush with the top of the embankment at track level.

Measure the width of the channel which has been cut from the embankment and trim a piece of card to fit the gap. Remove a section of the card which becomes the entrance; this example has a square top, but an arched entrance works well too. Measure and trim two wedge-shaped pieces of card for the angled walls.

Next place all the card components on to a piece of embossed plastic sheet which is lying face down on a flat surface, and carefully trim around the card using a very sharp blade, making sure that the courses of stone run parallel with the bottom of the walls. Before trimming, double check that the card is also 'face' down so the embossed stonework is on the outer side of the card.

Once the plastic sheet has been trimmed to size, the card and stone pieces are glued together using superglue. Two-millimetre thick coping stones have been fixed to the top of the walls. The underpass has been undercoated using grey aerosol paint, and glued into position in the embankment using superglue (*see* Fig. 387).

The terrain in front of the embankment is mainly flat, and the path running alongside the railway embankment has been marked into the terrain, as have the perimeters of the fields. A drainage gully,

Fig. 388: The underpass is carefully painted, dry-brushed and weathered to match the prototype stonework.

which will be kept dry, will separate the two fields, along with a hedge, fence posts and vegetation. The positions of all the fence posts have been carefully measured and marked on to the baseboard.

The walls bordering the track near to Irwell Vale Halt, and the underpass which the track runs over, are made from stone, which is now well weathered. The embossed plastic sheet on the underpass is painted to resemble the colour of the stone in the field trip photographs (*see* Fig. 388).

To achieve the look of these stones the whole structure is given a coat of mid-brown matt emulsion paint, which is left to dry. Successive coats of dirty brown emulsion paints are dry-brushed over the surface of the stonework to highlight individual stones and add detail to the walls of the underpass. Once the paints have dried, the whole structure is enhanced with thin washes and streaks of green paints and weathering powders.

The painting process of the underpass, or any walls for that matter, can be completed away from the layout before the construction of the terrain starts. This may make painting your stonework easier, especially if its location on the layout is a difficult place to reach with a paintbrush.

POST AND WIRE FENCING

Simple post and wire fences, like those in the field trip photographs, will be added to the layout in front of the path running along the embankment, along the front of the path, and to mark the perimeter of the individual fields. At this scale it isn't always necessary to add the wire, especially as the posts will be mostly obscured with grasses and weeds. Very fine fishing line held to the posts with superglue is an effective way of creating the wires for fences like the ones being modelled here.

The fence posts can be made with either plastic strip or wood. Cocktail sticks, which are approximately 2mm in diameter, are perfect for the creation of sturdy 6in posts in 'OO', or wooden skewers, which are approximately 3mm in diameter, and perfect for this type of fence post in 'O' gauge.

In this demonstration, the posts are to be just over a metre (4ft) above ground level, which is 16mm for 'OO' modellers. Measure approximately 25mm (1in) from the pointed end, and carefully trim with a sharp blade to give a flat end at the other.

The posts have been painted and allowed to dry (*see* Fig. 389). To paint the posts it is best to do them all together, so you achieve a fairly standard colour for them all. Put the trimmed cocktail sticks into a shallow container and add the paint, mixing the

Fig. 389: Cocktail sticks painted in large batches are a good source of fence posts.

Fig. 390: A spot of glue will hold the post firmly in place.

sticks around with a paintbrush. Don't use too much paint, just enough to cover the posts with a thin coat.

Fix the fence posts directly into the landscape either by pushing them into your terrain if the surface is soft, or by drilling small holes into it if necessary and inserting the posts, pointed end first. You will have 8–10mm of cocktail stick, which can be inserted into the ground to hold the post firm. A spot of PVA glue will help secure them (*see* Fig. 390). Posts that are too long or appear to taper at the bottom, can have their length altered by removing a little of the pointed end with a sharp blade.

The fence posts around the perimeter of the field and along the gully have each had a thin wash of paint applied to them whilst they were on the baseboard, just to weather them a little more than the fence running along the embankment; they can be weathered before they are fixed into the landscape if preferred.

ADDING THE TRACK

The track, which has been painted and lightly weathered away from the layout, is the next feature to be added to the landscape. Refer to your field trip photographs to see the level of weathering your own track will require. Further weathering will be applied to rails, sleepers and ballast after the ballast is fixed in place.

Fig. 391 shows the track after it has been pinned and glued in place. It is glued on to a length of 3mm thick card (which has been primed with PVA glue

Making an Embankment

Before adding the track, the foundation for the rear embankment is added to the terrain. A wedge-shaped piece of polystyrene, ceiling tile or a similar material can be used, but small embankments can also be made by trimming a number of wedge-shaped pieces of thick card or hardboard, trimmed to the angle at which you want the embankment to slope. Glue the wedges to the baseboard at 10–15cm (4–6in) intervals using superglue or PVA following the course of the embankment; allow for room at the front of the wedges for a strip of card to be glued to them.

Carefully measure the length of the front edge of the wedges and trim long strips of thick card or hardboard to the same measurement or slightly wider; the strips for this embankment have been trimmed slightly wider than the length of the front of the wedges to ensure the front edge of the timber on which the half-relief trees are fixed is hidden. Glue the strips to the fronts of the wedges and allow them to dry. The result is a very strong frame on which to add groundwork materials.

Although this method is perfect for long, straight embankments, when it is used for curved embankments the front pieces of card need cutting at angles to match the particular curve, which takes a little more planning. Glue the wedges in position, following the course that the embankment is running along, and allow them to dry. Cut pieces of card or hardboard slightly wider than the gap between two of the wedges, then place it flat over them. From behind, use a fine marker pen or pencil to mark the inner space between the wedges, then trim the card slightly wider than the pen lines so it fits just on the wedge, leaving some of it free for the next piece of card to sit on.

Once all the component pieces have been trimmed carefully, glue them to the tops of the wedges, creating a curved embankment; trim the bottoms of the card to fit the curve of the embankment.

Fig. 391: The painted and weathered track is fixed securely in place.

Fig. 392: Earth Powder is added on each side of the track, from the sleepers to the edge of the embankment.

beforehand to prevent it from lifting as the track dries), although cork sheet or foam underlay are a better option for operational model railways. The card is trimmed so that it is 8mm wider than the sleepers (4mm on each side), and its edges have been trimmed at an angle of approximately 45 degrees to create a realistically angled shoulder to the edge of the ballast. The PVA glue holding the track in place has been allowed to dry.

Earth Powder is added to each side of the track, from the very edge of the card underlay to the edge of the embankment (see Fig. 392). Some of the powder will eventually be covered by other scenic materials, but it acts as a suitable base for these. Diluted PVA, at a ratio of three parts water to one of glue, is used to hold the powder in place and is applied to the track side using a thick paintbrush. The powder is sprinkled on by hand, applying small pinches at a time as work along the track progresses. The powder will be seen to soak up the glue and will set into a durable surface.

Earth Powder is also added to the surface of the path which runs along the front of the embankment and disappears through the underpass, but here the addition of a few small, pale grey stones adds to the effect of a well-trodden surface. The surface of the path is made a little wider than it will ultimately be,

which allows for the edges of it to be blended into the surrounding landscape without losing the width of the path itself.

To enhance the track and to give it the appearance of the track in the field trip photographs, it has been ballasted using light grey ballast. Ballast plays an important part in the realism of track, and time and care should be taken over its laying (see Fig. 393).

First, take up small pinches of ballast with your index finger and thumb and carefully fill the spaces in between the sleepers. Ballast tends to look best when it ends flush with the top of the sleepers rather than covering them, which can look messy, but be guided by your own field trip photographs, as ballast and ash can sometimes cover sleepers obscuring them completely.

Next, take further pinches of ballast and add them in between the ends of the sleepers on the outside of the rails, again taking care not to add too much. Allow the ballast to cover the chamfered edge of the track underlay. For a very neat edge to the ballast it is good practice to work along the outer edge of it with a piece of timber, gently pushing the ballast back so it ends precisely along the edge of the card/cork underlay.

Finally, to hold the ballast in place, apply diluted PVA, at a ratio of three parts water to one of glue

Fig. 393: Take your time when adding the ballast to the track.

Fig. 394: Use sharp scissors to trim narrow strips of rubberized horsehair; these strips will be used for the hedges in the landscape.

and with a drop of washing-up liquid. Put the glue in a bottle fitted with a pointed nozzle, and very carefully apply it directly to the ballast in small drops: these will flow through the ballast and when dry will hold it firmly in place. Take care when ballasting around points and above point motors.

Although the hedges on the landscape will not be added to the scene until much later in the scenic process, it is a good idea to measure and trim the rubberized horsehair to size now. Use sharp scissors to trim long, narrow strips of fibres, and put them to one side for use later (see Fig. 394). The stone walls in the field trip photographs will be replaced with fence posts and hedges on the model, which is contradictory to some of the photographs but fits in nicely with the landscape around Irwell Vale.

Fig. 395: A blend of cement, Earth Powder, scatter and diluted PVA creates a great base on which to add scenic modelling materials.

TEXTURING THE FOREGROUND TERRAIN

Whilst the ballast is drying, the terrain towards the front of the layout is textured using a blend of cement, Earth Powder and scatter (for texture). The three materials are mixed into a runny paste using PVA glue, diluted three parts to one with water. The texturing layer is by no means absolutely critical, nor are the ratios of the mix, but applying it to your baseboards does give a good base coat on which to work, and extra detail to the surface of the landscape (see Fig. 395).

Apply a thin coat of diluted PVA to the baseboard just before adding the texture: this will make it easier to spread the paste. Use a wide paintbrush to apply the texturing to the baseboard (see Fig. 396). The textured undercoat is applied right up to and around

Fig. 396: Texture is applied to the fields using a wide paintbrush.

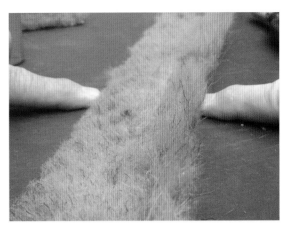

Fig. 397: The long fibres represent the long grass growing at the bottom of the embankment.

the fence posts as well as into the gully. When it has dried it will have sealed the edges of the gully, which will be necessary if you are considering adding a 'water' product into it.

A thin coat of emulsion paint is also useful for undercoating bare baseboards. Of course, any exposed areas of board can be covered with either the textured mix or a simple coat of emulsion paint.

EMBELLISHING THE EMBANKMENTS

Two pieces of Raw Grass (teddy-bear fur fabric) have been measured and trimmed to fit their location on the front embankment on each side of the underpass. Ideally cut these pieces very slightly longer and wider than their final size so they can be carefully trimmed to fit perfectly along the embankment and around any line-side features such as the underpass after they have been coloured and glued in place.

The fibres are trimmed to length using sharp scissors, and coloured using diluted Sap Green acrylic paint. Overall the length of the grass on the embankment will be fairly short, but leaving long fibres at the bottom of the strip creates the look of long grass running the length of the fence at the bottom of

the embankment (see Fig. 397). For a detailed demonstration of trimming and painting teddy-bear fur fabric, follow the procedures outlined in Chapters 2 and 3.

A piece of Raw Grass is also measured and trimmed to fit along the embankment to the rear of the scene. However, this section of the landscape is full of low-growing, ground-covering foliage, and the fabric here is treated slightly differently in that the fibres are mainly used as the stalks of the plants growing on the embankment. The fabric is trimmed with scissors, but the fibres are left fairly long so as to create depth to the foliage once scenic scatters have been added to it.

Paint the trimmed fabric in the same way as the previous piece, but apply not only green but also mid and dark brown acrylic or poster paints (see Fig. 398). The fabric can be sprayed with a suitable-coloured paint if you prefer, but if you use oil-based aerosol paints, be sure to allow them to dry before handling it as the fibres may stick together in an unsightly manner.

Fix the piece of Raw Grass to the rear embankment. To hold the grass sheet in place, use a paintbrush to apply a thin coat of PVA glue to the surface of the embankment. Press the sheet into it so the backing sheet comes into contact with the glue

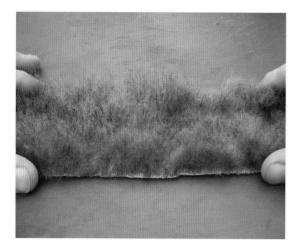

Fig. 398: Along with the green paint also add spots of brown and even black to the fabric for the rear embankment.

Fig. 399: Glue the fabric to the embankment, making sure it is pushed into the glue.

(see Fig. 399), and trim the sheet where necessary so it fits well along the track side. Any thin patches of fibre and the edge of the backing sheet will be hidden when the undergrowth is added to the embankment.

The green-coloured Raw Grass sheet can be glued to the front embankment using the same process as used for the brown-coloured sheet on the rear embankment; it, too, can be trimmed to fit if required. Be sure to work it right down to the base of the embankment so it butts up to the fence posts running along it (see Fig. 400). Note that some of the posts in the field trip photographs are almost completely hidden by long grass and weeds.

ADDING DETAIL TO THE LANDSCAPE

Where possible, especially if you are working on a wide baseboard, it is practical to start your scenic work towards the rear of the layout and to work forwards: this avoids your having to lean over freshly created scenery with the risk of damaging it. However, as the board in this case is only 60cm (2ft) wide, there is less chance of damage.

Apply a liberal misting of hairspray or diluted PVA to the fabric covering the rear embankment. Be sure

Making Up the Small Details

At this stage of the demonstration most of the terrain has been covered either with an under-coat of paint, a textured layer applied by brush, or painted fur fabric glued to the baseboard. These three elements are basically sub-surface layers on which to add scenic modelling materials, which make up the small details of the landscape.

Some of the techniques and materials outlined in the previous chapters can be used together and applied to the layout: for example scatters and static grass fibres blend well together, and long grass tufts can be added to short grass. The techniques and materials used for making tree canopies can be applied to ground-growing brambles, for example; this also ensures a visual continuity throughout your model landscape.

to mask off any surrounding areas you want to keep clear of the spray – for instance your track, the backscene or the electrics. Have to hand a selection of complementary-coloured scatters. Study your

Fig. 400: Most of the fence posts in the field trip photographs are obscured by long grass and weeds. Use the long fibres to mask some of the posts.

Fig. 401: A huge variety of weeds and plants can be seen growing on the rear embankment in the prototype photographs.

photographs to see how all the various plants grow together: is there a greater proportion of darker or lighter greens visible on the embankment? Where does the growth end in relation to the ballast? Are there any obvious gaps in the foliage, and does it grow right under the trees on the embankment?

With these details in mind, start applying the scatters by hand, using small pinches to build up the foliage, emulating the tones and textures seen on the prototype (see Fig. 401). A variety in the granule size of the scatters used will also add variety to the overall appearance of the embankment. More hairspray can be added to hold the scatters as you work along the embankment.

When you are happy with the coverage, spray diluted PVA evenly all over the scatters. Some of the scatter may be moved by this procedure, and if this creates unwanted gaps, then sprinkle a little more scatter on to those areas. A further misting of hairspray will help the scatter adhere to the fabric, and will dry into a very rigid surface.

More detail will be added to the undergrowth as work proceeds; for instance, there are a great many ferns evident in this photograph, and even a few weathered fence posts poking out from the general undergrowth.

THE FIELDS

A well grazed field contains very short grass, and our model field is covered using a blend of materials (see Fig. 402). First, take diluted PVA glue and use a wide paintbrush to apply it over the pre-textured or painted baseboard. Be sure to cover the whole of the 'field' with a liberal coating of glue, painting it right up to the fence posts around the perimeter of the field.

Using a very fine scatter, apply the first colour either directly by hand or with the use of a sieve. Apply a second, complementary colour either all over the field with a sieve or in small patches by hand. Work fairly swiftly, ensuring the glue is still wet. Further colours can be added to capture the appearance of the fields in your field trip photographs.

Small 'stones' – grey ballast works perfectly well – are added to the surface of the field to capture the look of the field trip photograph. Tiny pinches of Spring Meadow (1.5mm) static grass fibres are also sprinkled on to the glue by hand: not only will the fibres add to the overall texture of the field, they also help to blend it visually with the field next to it, and other parts of the landscape. The gully and other areas of the baseboard are also partially covered with

Fig. 402: Scatters, stones and short static grass fibres are added by hand to capture the look of the short-grass field.

Fig. 403: An assortment of static grass fibres is used to create the look of the recently mowed field and its surroundings.

the same materials during this step, as they will act as a good base on which to add other scenic materials.

The adjacent field, to the left-hand side of the underpass, is covered with static grass fibres applied using a Noch Gras-master applicator (see Fig. 403). First the surface of the field is given a thick coat of static grass glue, applied using a ½in paintbrush. It is advisable to work in relatively small areas at a time, rather than trying to cover large parts of the layout in one go. A metal hook is screwed into the surface, directly through the glue, and the crocodile clip attached to the applicator is attached to the hook (of course a nail can be used instead of a hook).

The first fibres added to the glue are medium-length Wild Grass beige (6mm). Follow the manufacturer's instructions supplied with your applicator, and make sure to choose the correct sieve for the length of fibres being used, to ensure you achieve the best results possible.

Next, Spring Meadow (1.5mm) fibres, the same as those added by hand to the adjoining scatter field, are added using the applicator. These fibres, which are not applied too thickly, are added to the glue whilst it is still wet. Applying different lengths and colours of fibre to the same field gives it a far more

realistic appearance, rather than just using one length and colour of fibre or scatter, especially when trying to capture the look and feel of natural landscapes.

Longer fibres, including Wild Grass (12mm), are added to the headland around the field, along the gully separating the two fields, and along the edge of the short-grass field; these blend the three features together.

A light sprinkling of Earth Powder applied between the fibres whilst the glue is still wet will mask any shine that may be present after the glue has dried. Allow the whole of the groundwork to dry before vacuuming up all the loose fibres and Earth Powder. More detail will be added to the fields as work proceeds.

Very finely chopped Raw Grass fibres are added to each side of the path in front of the embankment; they are sprinkled by hand on to a bed of freshly applied, diluted PVA glue, and worked into place using a pointed wooden skewer (see Fig. 404). The grass surrounding the path is fairly short and bright green in the prototype; later, the addition of longer tufts and other plants will blend together the edge of the path and the long grass running along the bottom of the embankment.

Fig. 404: Short fibres are added to the sides of the path to help blend it into the grass on the embankment.

Fig. 405: Hedges are a common sight throughout our landscape and add a great deal of interest to the layout.

PLANTING HEDGES

Hedges are a common sight bordering fields and properties all over the country (see Fig. 405). Sometimes fence posts can be seen among hedges, their wires invisible as they are masked by the fine branches in the hedge and the weeds and grasses growing along them.

The rubberized horsehair that was measured and trimmed earlier in the demonstration can now be transformed into realistic-looking hedges. The construction of hedges is covered in detail in Chapters 5, 6 and 7, but to recap: the rubberized horsehair is measured and trimmed to length. Depending on the style of the hedge being created, the horsehair is either pulled and teased apart to create a more open structure (for natural-looking hedges), trimmed into old-looking narrow hedges with gaps in them, or left neatly trimmed, which results in a far neater and manicured-looking hedge.

The hedge that runs partway along the embankment towards the right-hand side of the scene is fairly open in texture and tall. Tall hedges like this can be a useful addition to the scenery: not only do they look very effective bordering fields and lanes,

adding character to the scenery, but they can be especially useful if built tall enough to hide the point where trains leave the scene to enter a fiddle yard. Note, too, that sometimes small saplings can be seen growing out from the tops of older hedges, adding height to them and also providing a realistic, natural-looking feature to the scenery. It is not unusual to see huge dead tree trunks – the remains of a hedge-row tree – protruding from the tops of hedgerows.

The hedge enclosing the field to the left of the gully is styled on a fairly well maintained hedge, with some of its lower sections almost missing. The 'back' of the hedge, on the other side to the field, will be blended into the scenery as work progresses, which will make it look less like a strip of free-standing hedge and more like part of the natural scenery. A small gap has been created in the hedge with scissors to allow for a hedgerow tree to be inserted into it during a later step.

As well as hedgerow trees, small lengths of fencing, stone gateposts and timber styles are all little features that allow modellers to break up the monotony of hedges, walls and fences. Landscape features such as these can create the need for a path which can be added, thus adding further interest to the scene.

Fig. 406: A hedge is greatly improved if its base is blended into the surrounding landscape.

Fig. 407: Long grasses and weeds can often grow surprisingly tall along hedges and hedgerows.

BLENDING HEDGES INTO THE GROUNDWORK

Once the glue has dried, the bases of the hedges can be blended into the surrounding groundwork (*see* Fig. 406). This is an important step as it creates the impression that the hedges are actually growing in the landscape among the grass and other low-growing plants, rather than sitting on it. Before blending in the bottom of the hedge, the top of the hedge has been gently pulled to open up the structure a little.

Start the blending process by taking some diluted PVA glue on a small paintbrush and applying it liberally to the groundwork along the bottom of the hedge. Take some very finely chopped Raw Grass fibres and work them into the glue with a wooden skewer. Add a little fine scatter in random places beneath the hedge to emulate small plants growing around the base of the hedge. Earth Powder can be added to the glue too, and worked into the chopped fibres with the skewer. This method will also work equally effectively for blending buildings, walls and other scenic features into the landscape.

Sometimes long grass and foliage can grow a considerable way up the front of a hedge, masking its base completely, and if this is the look you are trying to create, use longer fibres and more foliage directly in front of the hedge instead of just underneath it

(*see* Fig. 407). Trim the fibres to an appropriate length, dip them in PVA, and position them close to the hedge, pushing them into the groundwork using a wooden skewer or similar.

Ready-made static grass tufts are also added to the short-grass field. To fix the tufts to the field, dip the base of each tuft into PVA glue and carefully position them in the field; pressing them down with a cocktail stick ensures they will be securely attached to the surface (Fig. 408). Look at your field trip photographs to see if they grow in groups or are they more spread out? The tufts around Irwell Vale grow in tightly packed groups but there are also the odd single tufts too.

To make your own tufts using static grass, take a sheet of acetate and place it on to a metal surface: a baking tray or the lid of a metal biscuit tin is ideal. Use a paintbrush or wooden skewer to apply small spots of static grass glue or neat PVA on to the acetate. Fill the hopper with a suitably coloured grass fibre of the correct length. Connect the crocodile clip from the applicator to the tin lid, turn the applicator on, and shake it over the drops of glue to create small tufts of fibres. When the glue is totally dry the tufts can be peeled away from the acetate and stuck to the groundwork with a tiny spot of glue.

Fig. 408: Static grass tufts, which are abundant in the prototype photographs, are added to the short-grass field.

Fig. 409: Low-growing weeds and plants on the embankment add to the overall groundwork – refer to your field trip photographs.

Although the embankment carrying the track looks natural in its present state, it can be made to look more like the overgrown embankment in the photographs taken at Irwell Vale with the addition of other scenic modelling materials.

For example, small pinches of canopy (synthetic hair) can be pulled off the plait and teased apart to form very open and airy structures, just like some of the tree canopies demonstrated earlier. The mounds of fibre are sprayed with hairspray and lightly sprinkled with an appropriate colour of scatter. Before applying the hairspray the teased-out fibres can be given a light spray of dark paint from an aerosol or airbrush, which will help strengthen them. With care, the hairspray can be applied directly over the wet paint, and the scatters added, all in one go.

The embankment in reference photograph Fig. 384 (see page 168) is almost completely covered with foliage, especially towards the bottom where it is bordered by the fence. A tiny amount of PVA is brushed on to the embankment in the places where the foliage is to be added. The mounds of foliage are carefully placed on to the glue and gently worked into it with a wooden skewer to ensure they adhere to the fabric on the embankment. The process can be repeated until the desired coverage has been achieved. Varying

and blending together different scatters can add to the overall appearance of the foliage.

Naturally sourced pieces of root that have been allowed to dry completely make very realistic dead trees, usually with a minimal amount of shaping required (see Fig. 410). A hole is made in the baseboard in the centre of the pre-cut gap in the hedge. The base of the 'tree' is dipped into glue and fixed into the hole in the baseboard. When you are happy with the angle of the tree, pull the hedge around the trunk so the tree appears to grow from the hedge

Fig. 410: Natural pieces of root can make very convincing dead trees.

Fig. 411: Pale-coloured dead grasses added to the groundwork introduce a nice contrast to the general greenery.

Fig. 412: Laser-cut paper or brass-etched plants add interest to the embankments.

itself. Of course, pieces of dead root can also be glued into the baseboard to represent free-standing trees. They can be painted or weathered prior to being fixed into the hedge if necessary.

Long grass and dead plant stems always seem to be in evidence regardless of the time of year, and their faded colour will add another element to the colour on the embankment. As with brambles and nettles, just a few small patches will improve the look of the foliage present by adding to the variety of texture and colour (see Fig. 411). For dead grasses use either long, straw-coloured static grass fibres or Raw Grass tufts cut off the sheet. Whichever material you choose, dip the bottom of the fibres in neat PVA (not diluted PVA, or the glue will get drawn up the fibres and stick them together) and push them into the embankment, working them into the undergrowth using a wooden skewer, cocktail stick or similar. The dead grass will add an interesting contrast in colour to the dark-leaved, half-relief trees after they are added on top of the embankment.

A couple of laser-cut ferns are added to the front and rear embankment (see Fig. 412). A small spot of glue will hold them in place among the other plants. Laser-cut plants can be lightly painted so they blend in with their surroundings.

TREES – ADDING HEIGHT

Trees and buildings set into the landscape are the best way of adding height to our layouts, not only to the foreground of the scene but also towards the back. Objects in the distance not only appear to get smaller as they get further away from the viewer, but in the case of trees they also appear to get denser. If you observe a row of trees in the distance or forest for that matter, all the tree canopies and various foliage textures appear to blend into one massive canopy held up by an assortment of trunks. As we look further into the trees even the trunks appear to blend into one another, until all we can see is a dark area beneath the trees.

Often trees in natural surroundings produce branches that grow very low down their trunks: this means that sometimes all we can see of groups of distant trees is a mass of foliage with no trunks visible at all. As modellers we can use this to our advantage, especially in situations such as the one being modelled in this demonstration. To the rear of the track at Irwell Vale there is a tall and dense row of trees: when scaled down in model form this row will make an impressive backdrop to the scene in front of it, and also add important height to the landscape; this in turn will demonstrate the true scale of the

Fig. 413: Trees can completely tower above everything around them, even telegraph poles, as shown here.

trees when compared to the trains running in front of them.

However, there are limitations to the size of the model trees we should add to our layouts; for instance, imagine a tree growing in the wild and standing 30–40m (100–130ft) in height. A tree around that height would need to be modelled, even in 'OO', standing at between 392–524mm (15–21in approximately). Common beech, English oak, horse chestnut, lime, London plane, poplar, Scots pine, silver birch and sycamore are relatively common trees, and all fall within these height boundaries when mature (see Fig. 413); and whilst this book is about scale modelling, trees built to these dimensions can look unrealistically large and should be scaled down a little. Of course in reality not *all* trees are that tall, and it is the choice of the individual as to how big they construct the trees on their layouts.

The row of half-relief trees demonstrated in Chapter 12 can now be added to the rear embankment (see Fig. 414). As already demonstrated,

Fig. 414: Half-relief trees take up minimal space at the rear of the layout and add height to the scene.

Fig. 415: An ivy-covered tree is placed behind the hedgerow at the bottom of the embankment on the right of the scene.

half-relief trees take up far less space on a layout than conventional trees. The piece of timber they are attached to can be either glued or screwed to the back of the baseboard, or simply placed in position, held in place between the rear embankment and the backscene, which will be added right at the end of the demonstration. If necessary, more foliage can be added to the tree armatures once they have been positioned; alternatively, small amounts of foliage can be removed or repositioned if required to allow for the clearance of the rolling stock.

The ivy-covered tree demonstrated in Chapter 10 has been given a light covering of scatter. In this landscape its planting pin has been inserted into a pre-drilled hole at the very bottom of the embankment behind the hedgerow on the right-hand side of the scene, hiding the point where the track leaves the layout (see Fig. 415).

The fallen, mostly dead tree constructed in Chapter 11 is added to the short-grass field (see Fig. 416). When adding features such as dead trees it is important to make the surrounding groundwork look natural, as though the tree has been there for some time, and not recently placed upon it. Blend the trunk and branches at ground level into the existing groundwork using materials already present in the field. A small hollow can be made in the ground where the roots once grew.

The silver birch demonstrated in Chapter 9 is added along the path behind the hedgerow (see Fig. 417). The groundwork between the hedge and the path has also been covered with a general carpet of growth, which helps to blend the back of the hedge into its surroundings.

To secure the oak tree (demonstrated in Chapter 8) into the layout, a hole is drilled into the baseboard

Fig. 416: There are plenty of dead and dying trees in the natural world. Including them in our landscape creates points of interest.

Fig. 417: A silver birch adds a contrasting-coloured trunk to the trees in the scene; this species is a common sight along the railway lines of Great Britain.

Fig. 418: A large oak tree is added to the left of the scene. Trees can be glued directly into the baseboard or held in place using planting pins.

Fig. 419: Tree roots look best when they are integrated into the surrounding groundwork.

and the planting pin is inserted into it, held in place with a spot of glue (see Fig. 418).

Alternatively, a piece of aluminium tube with an outer diameter of 6mm and an inner diameter of 4mm (4mm is the same diameter as the pin attached to the tree) can be glued into the hole using super-glue, and the tree's pin inserted into it. The planting pin ensures that trees are held firmly, and also that they can be repositioned in exactly the same place time after time. If multiple trees are constructed with planting pins of the same diameter, this introduces the option for moving trees periodically around the layout. Another benefit of using a metal planting pin is that the tree can be rotated a little at a time until the preferred 'front' of the tree faces the viewer.

It is important to blend the roots or trunk of the tree into the groundwork already in place on the layout (see Fig. 419). Taking time to complete this step can make all the difference between having a tree or trees that look as if they have simply been placed unrealistically on to the landscape, and having trees that actually look as if they are growing out from the ground with roots that hold them steady – which is exactly the same reason for blending the hedges into the landscape.

Glue can be used to hold the fibres blending the roots in place, but for trees that are likely to be removed from time to time it is best not to glue them down, because this allows for them to be lifted without causing any damage to the groundwork around the tree.

DETAILING THE LANDSCAPE

Model railway scenery can be improved and super detailed all the time; there is never a definitive point where our layouts can ever be called 'finished'. As a final treatment to the landscape it is good prac-tice to go over the whole layout with one or two scenic materials which can be applied to all parts of the scenery. This will give the landscape a common denominator, which will bring harmony to the scene.

Here, very lightly coloured, finely chopped Raw Grass fibres are added to the landscape to resemble random patches of dry grass: these are placed on the rear and front embankments, along the fences, around the path and underpass wall, around tree roots and around the fields (see Fig. 420).

To add the splash of colour evident in the pro-totype photographs, small patches of yellow, white and purple flowers are added to the fields, along the hedges, on the embankments and among the general undergrowth (see Fig. 421). Depending on the look you would like to create, the flowers can be applied

Fig. 420: By using a common material across the whole scene a balance can be created in all parts of the landscape.

Fig. 421: Small yellow, purple and white flowering plants are also added across the whole scene, and this helps to bring together all the various features within the diorama.

sparingly or heavily. The yellow flowers used here are actually fibres taken from a model rapeseed field from Noch, but they work perfectly well when pulled away from their backing and used in small clumps. Dip the bottoms of the fibres into PVA and carefully work them into the existing scenery. In the photographs taken around Irwell Vale, yellow flowers can be seen in both fairly dense and very light patches.

Coloured flowers applied throughout a scene will bring a hint of natural harmony between the background, middleground and foreground of any layout: apply coloured scatters or flowers randomly over the landscape, adding them more densely in some places than others, and not in equally spaced patches; like this, a natural-looking landscape will be created. The rosebay willowherb is made using static grass tufts that have had their tips coated with glue and dipped into a very fine coloured scatter.

ADDING A BACKSCENE

Adding a backscene to a layout or diorama will add to the realism of the overall landscape, creating perspective from the very front of the scene into the

Fig. 422: A pre-printed backscene, glued to a sheet of plyboard, is fixed behind the row of trees and completes the diorama.

far distance of the backscene (see Fig. 422). Ideally the colours in the backscene should complement the colours used in the foreground, and the two should blend together naturally. Even a plain board, painted sky blue and placed at the rear of a layout, will enhance the scenery in front of it and create a visual screen from all the things behind the scenic part of the layout.

THE FINISHED DIORAMA

By observing the details and the general feel for the landscape around Irwell Vale, a realistic-looking rural scene has been created. Many of the separate elements made throughout the book come together in the final scene, which captures many of the features in the field trip photographs.

Fig. 423: An overall photograph of the model which shows many of the elements in the field trip photographs recreated in 1:76 scale.

Looking over the fallen tree and through the half-relief trees into the backscene really gives an impression of depth to the landscape. Brightly coloured flowers and sun-bleached dead wood in the foreground add a contrast to the dark greens of the half-relief trees. An old tractor in the corner of the field adds a little colour and an interesting feature to the scene.

Fig. 424: Note the realistic height of the trees when compared to the DMU.

When looking down on to the track below as if from a bridge over the railway, the height of the trees in the scene can be appreciated. The neat shoulder of ballast can be seen here, as can a solitary old fence post on the embankment to the rear of the track.

Fig. 425: The colourful weed-covered embankment at the front of the track, complete with a stone underpass.

Note the variety in the colour and shape of the plants and weeds growing on the embankment: all the elements of the landscape blend into each other naturally, with no obvious joins between the various materials and features of the scene.

Fig. 426: A gently curving hedge surrounds the freshly cut field. The fields at the front of the diorama are separated by a dry gully.

A general view of the landscape, showing the subtle colour changes within it.

Fig. 427: Large trees or groups of trees are a good option for hiding the entrance to fiddle yards.

Not only do large trees make a striking addition to our model railway layouts, they are also very good at hiding the point where trains leave the scenic part of the railway. Trees in front of railway tracks also add interest to the layout in general and can help frame the scene behind them, as in this demonstration, where the trees to the left and right of the scene create a 'window' through which to watch the trains go by.

Fig. 428: All the elements blend together to create a natural-looking scene.

Natural materials can make a surprisingly effective addition to our models, as can be seen here in the form of this dead hedgerow tree which was originally a piece of tree root. Note how open the canopy of the silver birch tree in the foreground is compared to the trees in the background.

Fig. 429: OO gauge – 'Irwell Vale'. Class 25 No. 25 279 hauls a short train through Irwell Vale and over a stone-built underpass. The two fields in front of the embankment are separated by a narrow gully which is bordered with long grass, weeds and colourful plants. The field to the right, bordered by a simple fence, is well grazed and kept very short but contains long tufts and an old tree, which although mostly dead still struggles to survive. The field to the left is bordered by a mature hedge which includes the remains of an old hedgerow tree; the field itself contains long grass. To the rear of the scene in front of the backscene is a tall row of dense trees which creates a suitable screen for the trains to run in front of. Note the dead tree and the gap in the foliage that its leafless form creates. A splash of colour and movement is provided by the old tractor left to the elements in the corner of the field, and the dog that barks at it. (Here the overall scale of everything in the scene is apparent when compared to the class 25 locomotive.). Modelling railways needn't be all about the railway itself, as can be seen here: the railway is just a small part of the scenery, even in a close-up photograph like this.

Fig. 430: Our scenic journey comes to an end. The final field trip photograph, showing many of the features captured in the diorama.

MANUFACTURERS AND SUPPLIERS

BACHMANN EUROPE PLC
Moat Way
Barwell
Leicester
LE9 8EY
Tel: 0870 751 9990
E-mail: sales@bachmann.co.uk
Website: www.bachmann.co.uk

DAPOL
Dapol Ltd
Gledrid Industrial Park
Chirk
Wrexham
LL14 5DG
Tel: +44 (0) 1691 774455
E-mail: Shop@dapol.co.uk
Website: www.dapol.co.uk

DELUXE MATERIALS
Realistic water materials and modelling glues
E-mail: info@deluxematerials.com
Website: www.deluxematerials.com

DOVEDALE MODELS
Handmade buildings
David Wright
6 Ivy Court
Hilton
Derby
DE65 5WD
Tel: +44 (0) 1283 733547
E-mail: david@dovedalemodels.co.uk
Website: www.dovedalemodels.co.uk

HORNBY
Customer Care
Hornby Hobbies Ltd
Westwood Industrial Estate
Margate
Kent
CT9 4JX
Tel: +44 (0) 1843 233525
E-mail: customercare@hornby.com
Website: www.hornby.com

id Backscenes
24 School Road
Telford
TF7 5JG
Tel: +44 (0) 7970 678753
E-mail: info@art-printers.com
Website: www.art-printers.com

JAVIS MANUFACTURING LTD
JBB House, 6 Hammond Avenue
Whitehill Industrial Estate
Reddish, Stockport
SK4 1PQ
Tel: +44 (0) 161 480 2002
E-mail: p-bridge@btconnect.com
Website: www.javis.co.uk
Trade sales only

METCALFE
Bell Busk
Skipton
North Yorkshire
BD23 4DU
Tel: +44 (0) 1729 830072
E-mail: info@metcalfemodels.com
Website: www.metcalfemodels.com

NOCH
Static grass, Gras-master applicator and laser-cut plants
Noch GmbH & Co. KG
Lindauer Straße 49
D – 88239 Wangen im Allgäu,

Germany
Tel: (+49) 7522 9780–28
Fax: (+49) 7522 9780–80
E-mail: noch@noch.de
Website: www.noch.de or www.noch.com
Distributed in the UK by Gaugemaster Controls Ltd,
Arundel
www.gaugemaster.com

P&D MARSH Model railways
Pre-painted white metal figures and accessories
The Stables
Wakes End Farm
Eversholt
Milton Keynes
MK17 9FB
Tel: +44 (0) 1525 280068
E-mail: paul@pdmarshmodels.com
Website: www.pdmarshmodels.com

PECO
PECO Technical Advice Bureau
Underleys
Beer
Devon
EX12 3NA
Tel: +44 (0) 1297 21542
E-mail: info@pecobeer.co.uk
Website: www.peco-uk.com

SANKEY SCENICS
16 Norbreck Close
Great Sankey

Warrington
Cheshire
WA5 2SX
Tel: +44 (0) 7565 892209
E-mail: sankeyscenics@live.co.uk
Website: www.sankeyscenics.co.uk

SKYTREX (2013) Ltd
OO accessories and buildings
Unit 1
Charnwood Business Park
North Road
Loughborough
LE11 1LE
Tel: 01509 213789
E-mail: sales@skytrex.com
Websites: www.skytrexmodelrailways.com
        www.ogauge.co.uk

TREEMENDUS
Scenic modelling materials, handmade trees, scenery and dioramas
TREEMENDUS
112 Church Lane
Ashton on Mersey
Sale
Cheshire
M33 5QG
Tel: +44 (0) 161 973 2079
E-mail: info@treemendus-scenics.co.uk
Website: www.treemendus-scenics.co.uk

INDEX